ENJOY
your Middle
Schooler

ENJOY your Middle Schooler

A Guide to Understanding the Physical, Social, Emotional, and Spiritual Changes of Your 11–14 Year Old

Wayne Rice

ZondervanPublishingHouse

Grand Rapids, Michigan

A Division of HarperCollinsPublishers

Enjoy Your Middle Schooler
Copyright © 1994 by Wayne Rice

Requests for information should be addressed to:
Zondervan Publishing House
Grand Rapids, Michigan 49530

Library of Congress Cataloging-in-Publication Data

Rice, Wayne.
  Enjoy your middle schooler : a guide to understanding the
  physical, social, emotional, and spiritual changes of your 11–14
  year old / Wayne Rice.
     p. cm.
  ISBN 0-310-40581-5
  1. Child psychology. 2. Middle-school children—Psychology.
3. Puberty. I. Title.
HQ772.R44   1994
305.23'55—dc20   93-38537
                                                              CIP

Edited by Bruce and Becky Durost Fish
Cover design by Sarah J. Slattery
Cover photo by Super Stock

Printed in the United States of America

94 95 96 97 98 / ML / 10 9 8 7 6 5 4 3 2 1

To Nathan, Amber, and Corey

CONTENTS

INTRODUCTION

When your child . . .

Goes into the bathroom and locks the door . . .
Asks you to drop him off a block away from the school . . .
Can't find her homework, but knows exactly where to find her comb . . .
Is absolutely positive he knows more than you about everything . . .
Complains that she can't figure out how to operate the washing machine, but is an expert at operating the VCR . . .
Spends two minutes talking with you after school, but two hours on the phone with a friend just seen at school . . .
Complains that school, church, and family activities are boring . . .
Decides to decorate his bedroom in "early landfill" . . .
Answers all questions with "I dunno" or "Nuthin' " . . .
Changes her mood from incredible joy to intense depression—in five minutes . . .
Spends an hour getting dressed just to take out the trash . . .

. . . Congratulations! Chances are you're the parent of a middle schooler—an eleven- to fourteen-year-old who is leaving behind his or her childhood and beginning the rapid journey of adolescence that leads to adulthood.

Adolescence is an adventure for children, but it can be even more of an adventure for parents who don't know what to expect. You probably went to a junior high school or an elementary school that included seventh, eighth, and possibly ninth grade. Today, most American students leave

9

elementary school when they complete fifth grade. They spend their early adolescent years in middle school. It's a new experience for them, and a new experience for their parents.

I began working with middle schoolers in 1963 and continued doing so for more than a decade. I became something of an expert in youth ministry circles on this age group. Yet when my children became middle schoolers, I was apprehensive and unsure of myself. That's when I decided that early adolescence is a lot like childbirth.

When my wife, Marci, was pregnant with our first child, Nathan, I was filled not only with anticipation, but also with fear. We had heard a few, unsettling horror stories and had a lot of questions and fears. What could we do to insure that our baby would survive? What would our baby look like? Would he or she be healthy? How would this baby change our lives? Would we be able to provide what our baby needed?

In many ways, I experienced the same feelings when Nathan became a middle schooler. He was experiencing a second birth—his birth into adulthood. I had the same questions and worries I had before: What could we do to make sure he survived? What would he look like? Would he be healthy? How would this experience change our lives?

Just as Marci and I were able to relax during Nathan's first birth (thanks to Lamaze classes and the help of doctors and friends), we were also able to relax during his second birth—early adolescence. We didn't attend any Lamaze classes for parents of young teens, but we were able to draw upon our experience of working with middle schoolers. It helps when you know what to expect.

That's the purpose of this book. It is designed to help you relax and understand some of the things that are happening in the life of your middle-school son or daughter. When you know what to expect, you can enjoy your child's middle-school years rather than suffer through them.

I am grateful to God that all three of my children have

successfully navigated the rough waters of early adolescence and are now well on their way to adulthood. It's been a joy to watch them grow and change, although I don't want to downplay the difficult times of stress and crisis. God has been good to our family.

It would be nice if there were a set of fool-proof formulas to make successful parents of us all, but there aren't. Any number of variables can impact the process significantly, and many of them are out of our control.

Two variables that have made me look good as a parent are (1) three great kids and (2) a wonderful wife. Marci has been a far better mom to our kids than I have been a dad, I'm afraid. Another variable for which I am grateful is my church. The people of Community Covenant Church in Lakeside, California, have loved my children and given them a safe place to both be themselves and discover the meaning of the Gospel.

A special word of thanks to my friend Dave Lambert at Zondervan Publishing House for suggesting that I write this book. He edited *Junior High Ministry*, a book of mine for youth workers, and felt that a similar book for parents would be worthwhile.

It is my prayer that this book will be an encouragement to you and that in some small way it will help you and your children enjoy this important time of life.

CHAPTER 1

The Wonder Years

Comedian Andy Griffith is famous for his deadpan description of a football game as seen for the first time through the eyes of a country bumpkin.

> There was all these people sittin' around this great big cow pasture, just a-hollerin' and a-yellin' at all these big fellers who were a-kickin' and a-throwin' this pumpkin up and down the pasture. And then all of a sudden, a bunch of convicts in striped shirts started wavin' their arms and a-blowin' whistles.

Griffith's account of a football game is not unlike the way some people describe middle schoolers, kids between the ages of eleven and fourteen. They observe what appear to be children acting like adults, or adults acting like children, or human beings acting like aliens from outer space. They are mystified by it all. This is especially true for adults whose oldest children are entering early adolescence. Just as it is impossible to appreciate a football game without having some knowledge of the rules, so it is difficult to appreciate and enjoy what is taking place in the life of a middle schooler without having some knowledge of what to expect.

Worse than ignorance of what to expect, however, is believing things that are not true. There is a widespread myth believed by many parents. Called the myth of the teenage werewolf, its message is "no matter how pleasant and sweet and innocent your child might be as a youngster, as soon as the first hormonal surge of puberty occurs, that beautiful child will inevitably turn into an uncontrollable monster who will wreak havoc on your home and personal lives for a decade or more."[1] This myth strikes fear into the hearts of parents and makes good parenting almost impossible.

The myth of the teenage werewolf is, of course, only a myth—a terrible stereotype that is grossly unfair and unrepresentative of the vast majority of young adolescents. Variations of the myth have been around for decades. Mark Twain is quoted as saying, "When a child turns thirteen, parents should put him in a pickle barrel, nail the lid shut, and feed him through a knothole. Then—when he turns sixteen—plug up the knothole."

Adolescent bashing still makes for good humor, but it produces anxiety rather than laughter among parents who have come to believe the myth. I met one newly-married couple who glumly insisted that they were not going to have any children—simply because they were unable to deal with the prospect of their children growing up to become teenagers.

Adolescence has always been a difficult time of change and adjustment for both parents and children. Parents of the past knew that when their children reached adolescence, there would be a certain amount of disharmony and rebellion to deal with. But the idea that children at puberty would be transformed into frightening and uncontrollable presences in the home did not capture the public imagination until recently.

What has given rise to this negative perception of adolescence? It can be partially traced to cultural phenomena such as the drug epidemic of the sixties and seventies, the image of rebellious teenagers in films and television, the breakdown of authority in society, and the alarming rise of teenage pregnancies, suicides, and gang violence. But while this litany of bad news is cause for great concern, it is important to keep in mind that the actual number of young people who become seriously involved in drugs, crime, or other types of aberrant behavior is a small fraction of the total age group. Most teenagers not only survive their adolescent years without doing serious harm to themselves or others, but they prosper during that time and develop into healthy, well-adjusted adults.[2]

There is no good reason for you to believe the myth of the teenage werewolf or any of its variations. If you do, you will risk making a self-fulfilling prophecy of it. When we expect the worst from our kids, we usually get it.

Most people (children included) tend to live down to our expectations. That's why it's important for us to understand early adolescence. If we know and understand the truth, our expectations will be realistic, allowing us to encourage our children toward a healthy adulthood and helping us enjoy their middle-school years along with them.

Understanding Is the Key

Twelve-year-old Alicia's parents were worried. Instead of spending time with the family, Alicia disappeared into her bedroom every night and closed the door. Her parents were afraid that she was becoming depressed and withdrawn, and they suspected that she might be doing something they did not approve of.

Alicia spent hours alone in her room, whispering on the phone, quietly doing her homework, listening to music. Sometimes a friend or two would come over and join Alicia in her bedroom retreat. To Alicia's parents, this behavior seemed unusual and somewhat rebellious. They delivered an ultimatum: Either she stopped closing her bedroom door or they would remove it from its hinges. Alicia stormed out of the house in tears, screaming, "You just don't understand! I hate you!"

Alicia was right. Her parents didn't understand. When her mother told me about this incident later, I explained a few things about normal adolescent development. By the end of our conversation, she was beginning to understand why her daughter needed her privacy so much—why it was so important to her.

Alicia's parents aren't alone. Countless parents are totally unprepared for the changes that will take place in their children when they reach early adolescence. They are unprepared because they lack understanding.

You need to understand what is going on in the life of your middle-school child. Most parents do not. To the average adult, middle-school children are incredibly strange people and virtually impossible to understand. They are moody, noisy, unreasonable, disrespectful, irreverent, lazy, and just plain obnoxious most of the time. But from the perspective of the young adolescent, there are good reasons behind all these idiosyncrasies that drive adults crazy. What is needed is the ability to understand. Without it, communication and good relationships become almost impossible.

I don't want to give the impression that understanding middle schoolers is easy. Frankly, there are some things about this age group that defy understanding. But contributing to the problem is the fact that we adults are often so far removed from our own adolescence that we no longer remember what those years were like. We can't remember. And since we don't spend a lot of time around young adolescents to learn by observation, we are left vulnerable to the myth.

Theoretically, every adult has one good point of identification with middle schoolers—he or she was once the same age. Even though today's kids are growing up in a different world, most of the problems they face are not that different from those we faced at their age. You'd think that we would have some empathy with our kids because we've experienced the same problems.

But psychologists tell us that a serious problem exists when adults try to remember what being between the ages of eleven and fourteen was like. The problem is repression, a kind of adult amnesia. Repression is defined as the "rejection from consciousness of painful or disagreeable ideas, memories, and feelings."[3] To make life more endurable, the brain tries to forget, or at least block from memory, painful experiences. Those experiences are never lost completely from consciousness; they are simply pushed back into the recesses of the mind and rarely, if ever, recalled. Therapists commonly use hypnosis or some other method to help people recall and deal with repressed events.

What does this have to do with understanding middle schoolers? Psychologists agree that many of life's most painful experiences occur during the middle-school years. If you are thinking, *I don't remember those years being all that painful,* you prove my point. You don't remember! You don't remember the embarrassment and humiliation of having to dress for that first Phys. Ed. class; the struggle with parents for independence; the times when you were not accepted into the right group of kids; guilt feelings brought on by a new awareness of your sexuality; puzzling questions from a developing mind; love triangles and broken hearts. We don't want to go through life with all that on our minds, so we repress those experiences. We have a difficult time understanding middle schoolers because our tendency is to forget, to repress.

One educator has compared early adolescence with the experience of childbirth.

> But where is one who does not wince at the memory of his adolescence? . . . Women say they cannot remember the pangs of childbirth. Crafty nature blots them out, lest there be no more children. So also—one does not remember one's second birth, from childhood into youth. This second birth becomes in memory a dull pain.[4]

If you can't remember your adolescence, you will have a hard time developing a good relationship with your kids during theirs. It is difficult, if not impossible, to have a positive relationship with people you don't understand. You tend to avoid them, or control them, or put them down. It's no wonder that many adolescents feel avoided, controlled, and put down by the adults in their lives.

All this can be avoided through understanding. The best way for you to understand your middle-school children is to get in touch with your own adolescent years. In other words, remember. Sure it's hard to reach back and recall events and feelings from those years, but it isn't impossible, and it does wonders to help you empathize with your kids. Understanding middle schoolers does not mean becoming an expert on youth or youth culture; it means developing a good memory. Your memory can be one of your greatest resources as a parent.

In my office, I have a framed portrait of myself when I was in the eighth grade. That picture helps me remember that I went through the same kinds of experiences my children are going through. Many times I have looked into the face of my son or daughter and felt like I was looking into a mirror. I recognized myself as a boy around that age. That realization has helped me tremendously as a parent.

You may be thinking, *Yes, but kids are so different today. What good does it do for me to remember my adolescence when today's children are nothing at all like children of a generation ago?*

It is true that today's kids are growing up in a different environment—a different world. But in most other respects, they are more the same than they are different. Today's young adolescents are asking the same fundamental questions: Who am I? Why am I here? What am I going to do with my life? These are questions of identity, purpose, and meaning. Young adolescents are no more troublesome and annoying to parents today than they have ever been.

Consider this description of young people: "Youth today love luxury. They have bad manners, contempt for authority, no respect for older people, and talk nonsense when they should be working. Young people do not stand up any longer when adults enter the room. They contradict their parents, talk too much in company, guzzle their food, lay their legs on the table, and tyrannize their elders." An indictment of teens by one of today's conservative leaders? Hardly. That quote is attributed to Socrates, who lived more than five hundred years before Christ. Perhaps kids in ancient Greece weren't all that different from kids today.

Here's another quotation about adolescence: "The world

is passing through troubled times. The young people of today think of nothing but themselves. They have no reverence for parents or old age; they are impatient of all restraint. They talk as if they knew everything, and what passes for wisdom with us is foolishness to them. As for the girls, they are forward, immodest, and unwomanly in speech, behavior, and dress." This biting critique is from Peter the Hermit, the fiery monk who spearheaded the First Crusade in A.D. 1095. Apparently, he had as much difficulty understanding medieval kids as we do the current crop.

My point is simply this: There is nothing wrong with today's youth that a little understanding can't remedy. There is no reason to fear adolescence or to make it any more difficult for your kids than it already is. Adolescence is not pathological. It is an exciting and wonderful time of life—a sacred journey from childhood into adulthood that every human being makes. You survived, and chances are excellent that your child will, too. It helps to remember that.

If your memory won't cooperate, it's not likely that you will need to go to a psychiatrist for therapy. Simply being more observant of your own children will often do the trick. You might talk to people who knew you well when you were in the sixth or seventh grades (like your parents, if possible). Sometimes it's helpful to write down as much as you can remember about those years.

Keep in mind that the reason for all this remembering is to better understand young adolescents and identify with their problems, concerns, and feelings. Otherwise, parenting becomes seriously complicated, and communication becomes very difficult.

Young adolescents frequently exaggerate their miseries and overdramatize their suffering. It's hard to be supportive and helpful when deep down we don't believe things are as bad as they let on. But their suffering is very real, and a purely adult perspective is the last thing they need in a moment of crisis. Like any person in difficulty, adolescents need someone who will listen and understand. When your child tells you that she is the ugliest girl in the whole class, believe it. You have been given an important piece of information. Your acceptance must come first; advice, reason, and perspective can come later.

Like many kids going through puberty, I had my share of romantic experiences. Whenever I fell in love with the girl who sat on the other side of the classroom or the pastor's daughter or whoever the lucky girl happened to be, I was certain that it was the real thing. Someday we would get married, have kids, and live happily ever after.

My parents never took these love affairs seriously. They would shake their heads and call it "puppy love." I can't describe the pain and anger that their apparent indifference created in me. In retrospect, they were right. But at the time, their lack of understanding hurt deeply. I wish they had understood that for puppies, puppy love is very real.

A Time of Transition

I am convinced that early adolescence is the most critical time of a person's life. Every stage of life is significant and brings its own set of problems and benefits, but there is no time of life which compares with early adolescence in terms of developmental change. It is critically important in transitioning from childhood to adulthood.

I read a story in the newspaper a few years ago about a German man who was traveling to Oakland, California. He bought a ticket in Frankfurt, Germany, to Los Angeles International Airport, with a short connecting flight to Oakland. When he arrived in Los Angeles, he asked someone at the ticket counter where the flight to Oakland could be boarded. Because of the traveler's poor English, the person at the counter thought he said "Auckland." Incredibly, the traveler mistakenly boarded a plane for Auckland, New Zealand, instead of Oakland, California, and the mistake was not noticed until fifteen hours later when he found himself halfway around the world in a country he had no desire to visit.

When I read that article, I was reminded of what sometimes happens during early adolescence. In many ways, childhood is like that flight from Frankfurt to Los Angeles. Then come the early adolescent years (the airport terminal), and in the confusion of it all, many kids get on the wrong airplane. The moral of the story is to watch your connections. Changes can be very important, not only in airports, but in life, and some of the biggest changes in a person's life take place during the middle-school years.

What are those changes? The most obvious, of course, is puberty—a person physically changes from a child into an adult. But there are many other changes as well: social, intellectual, emotional, and spiritual.

Puberty is all about change. I heard one person describe it as "when massive doses of progesterone and testosterone come roaring into the body, setting off a biophysical disaster of unprecedented proportions." Misconceptions abound regarding puberty. It is not a disease, so it doesn't need a cure. Everyone experiences it, which means that it's perfectly normal, even though it often results in what appears to be unusual or abnormal behavior.

It is not uncommon, for example, for middle schoolers to catch a sudden case of the giggles or to erupt into tears without warning. They may be bursting with energy one moment and for no apparent reason become lethargic and lazy the next. They will sometimes act like adults and at other times act like children. They may become unusually preoccupied with the mirror and worry to the point of depression about every supposed defect in their physical appearance. They may decide to do something one moment and then immediately change their minds and do precisely the opposite. None of this is what one would call normal behavior, but it is helpful to remember that with this age group, the abnormal is normal a good deal of the time.

For some middle schoolers, the new experiences and

problems they encounter during puberty will be mild and go practically unnoticed by the casual observer. But for other kids, puberty creates some serious difficulties, and many of them will be completely unable to cope. Erik Erikson wrote that it is not until adolescence that the individual begins to see himself as having a past and a future that are exclusively his. Early adolescence is thus a pivotal time of both review and anticipation, with corresponding feelings of confusion, doubt, and worry.[5]

It is during these years that our kids will do everything they can to discard their childhood in an attempt to become unique individuals. Often these efforts result in frustration and failure. As the emerging adults try to break away from parental domination—to seek autonomy and a degree of independence—complications arise. Parents are naturally reluctant to let go, and they often don't understand what is going on. Meanwhile, the middle schoolers are certain that they are not being allowed to grow up and that the only possible solution is to rebel.

During the early adolescent years, the juvenile crime rate soars. There is much in the news these days about teenage runaways, teenage drug abusers, teenage pregnancy, and teenage suicide, and much of that news is about kids under the age of fifteen. The evidence is clear: The early adolescent years are pivotal and uniquely troublesome, requiring more, not less, of our concern and attention.

Ironically, some parents neglect their children and pay less attention to them when they reach this stage of life. They argue that since young adolescents are in transition—neither children nor adults—the best approach is to wait for them to grow out of it, wait for them to grow up and settle down into something we are more comfortable with.

But kids don't grow out of it. The changes that take place during early adolescence and the supervision and guidance (or lack of it) that they receive during this time leave an indelible mark on their lives. The experiences of early adolescence are life shaping and life changing. As Erikson said, "The growth events of early adolescence are in large measure determined by what has happened before and *determine much of what follows* [emphasis mine]."[6] This is why early adolescence occupies such a pivotal position in a person's life.

A Time of Questioning

When she was a little girl, Amy loved going to Sunday school and church services with her family. She enjoyed the activities, the singing, the stories that were told. But now, at age fourteen, Amy finds church *bor-r-ring* and religion no longer relevant. "I just don't think I believe that stuff any more," she says. "When I was younger, everything seemed to make sense to me. I believed that God was in control of everything and that there was a good reason for everything that happens. Everything was going to work out fine. But then my family started having problems, and some of my friends at church told lies about me. I just don't know. It all used to be so neat and tidy, but now it seems totally ridiculous."

Amy is not unlike many young adolescents who are calling into question what they were taught as children. Childhood myths begin to crumble as children who are becoming adults discover new ways of perceiving reality. They no longer accept everything their parents or teachers tell them. Now they want to understand things for themselves and learn things on their own. In addition, with new reasoning abilities, they find it hard to reconcile what they have been taught with the experiences that they and others are having. Sometimes a distressing situation like a divorce in the family or a death or, as in Amy's case, friends who are hurtful, can cause a crisis of faith and seriously shake the foundations of belief.

It is not uncommon for middle schoolers to temporarily suspend or reject entirely the values and beliefs they acquired during childhood. This questioning continues until they are able to determine whether these values and beliefs have any validity or relevance to their young adult lives. Just as Santa Claus and the stork were discarded years earlier, so the God of the Old Testament and the Christ of the New may not be quite as believable as they once were. This is no reason to panic. It's a necessary step that young people take in order to arrive at a faith and value system which are their own, rather than their parents'.

Again, we need to recognize that the middle-school years are critical—when much of this questioning and doubting takes place. The only way we can improve the chances that our children's faith will survive somewhat intact is to keep the relationship with our kids warm and keep the communication lines open.

Parents often become frustrated with their middle-school children because they typically get very argumentative at this age. "They snarl at everything I say." "They just won't take no for an answer." "They want to argue about everything!" In most cases, kids are not simply being belligerent. They are trying to better understand the world they live in. This sometimes takes the form of arguing with or challenging their parents and other authority figures. It is normal for kids at this age to act as if they know everything and to insist that their parents know nothing. It doesn't help to try to convince them otherwise.

When your middle schoolers argue with you, the best strategy is to try to be understanding and remain calm. Enter into reasoned discussions rather than shouting matches. Listen carefully, respond appropriately, and don't expect agreement or compliance on every issue. Allow your kids the room to challenge you and to arrive at conclusions which make sense to them for the time being.

Some very significant thinking and learning is going on at this age. Don't expect middle schoolers to have all their ideas neatly organized and their conclusions finalized. There's a lot of internal questioning going on. Don't assume that your children's brains have stopped working simply because they communicate in shrugs and grunts. Young adolescents rarely have the confidence they need to express their questions, doubts, and intellectual struggles. But these problems exist, and they play an important role in shaping middle schoolers' values and beliefs. Their questioning should be encouraged and celebrated rather than reprimanded and put down.

A Time of Openness

One of the primary reasons why the middle-school years have been called "The Wonder Years" is that young adolescents are extremely open to new ideas and experiences. The world of adulthood is opening up to them, and their eyes are wide open. They want to try everything, to experience everything, to believe every new idea that comes along. They are open to good ideas and bad ideas, positive behaviors and negative ones. They are in the middle of a complicated trial-and-error process of identity formation which will help determine what kind of person they will eventually be.

Twelve-year-old Darrin isn't sure what he wants to be. After he saw the Dead Freaks rock group at a concert, he just knew that he wanted to play drums in a heavy-metal band. He bought a Dead Freaks T-shirt at the concert and decorated his room with Dead Freaks posters and stickers. But a few weeks later, Darrin's shop teacher at school told him that the mahogany chessboard he had made in class was outstanding and suggested that Darrin enter it in the fair. Darrin began thinking that maybe he would save his money for carpenter's tools and wood rather than drums.

At home, Darrin's parents are frustrated and confused by Darrin's behavior. When he was told that they were going to visit Uncle Art and Aunt Barb for the weekend, he seemed agreeable to the idea because Uncle Art sometimes takes him fishing in the lake near their home. But when Friday arrived, Darrin refused to go, insisting that Uncle Art and Aunt Barb were "boring and stupid." Darrin locked himself in his room, where posters of the Dead Freaks have been replaced by photos of country singer Garth Strait.

Darrin's unpredictable behavior may frustrate his parents, but it is not at all unusual for a middle schooler. Kids this age will often buy into things one day that they discard the next for something completely different. They will act out a particular role or behave in a way that coincides with how they want to be and how they want others to view them—on that particular day. They often want to see how others will respond. If they don't like the feedback or if they get bored with the whole thing, they will often discontinue the behavior and seek out some alternative. This is why middle schoolers' personalities can change from one week to the next. The things they wanted to do last week no longer interest them this week. The activities that were "cool" last week are "totally bogus" this week. Such apparently inconsistent behavior is part of an important growing-up process. For middle schoolers, life is one big jigsaw puzzle with many pieces missing. Their job is to find the pieces and put them into place.

Senior-high students, by comparison, are nearing the completion of this process and will often be extremely set in their ways. Normally, by the time teenagers graduate from high school, they have adopted the personality, lifestyle, and values that will be theirs for the rest of their lives.

I have attended several of my high school reunions for the Camarillo High School class of '63. It is always good to see my old friends again, but at times it is also eerie. I get the feeling that I have been put into a time machine, taking me back to 1963. Everyone is so much the same. (I commented to my wife that I felt like I was at a high school masquerade party where everyone was disguised as an old person.)

With few exceptions, I could have made very accurate predictions in 1963 as to what my senior classmates would become ten or even twenty-five years down the road. The introverts were still introverts; the extroverts were insurance salesmen or politicians; the high achievers were successful in business or in education; the class clowns were still clowns.

This is in stark contrast to the openness of younger teens. Trying to pin them down or make generalizations about them is like trying to nail Jell-O to a wall. They remain open to all kinds of possibilities for their lives. The only predictable thing about them is their unpredictability.

One explanation for the openness of middle schoolers is offered by educator H. Stephen Glenn, who suggested that children develop their values and beliefs in a cyclical manner.[7] This chart describes the cycle:

Cycle One:
Age 0-4	Discovery
Age 5-8	Testing Out
Age 9-12	Concluding

Cycle Two:
Age 12-14	Discovery
Age 15-17	Testing Out
Age 18+	Concluding

According to Glenn, the first stage in cycle one is a time of discovery for the very young child, when the world is being explored for the first time. That's why you have to kid-proof your house when these little tykes are around. Newborns to four-year-olds are at great risk because they are constantly sticking things into their mouths, crawling into places they don't belong, and scaring parents out of their wits.

The second stage is a time of testing out (age five to eight), when knowledge is tested on others to determine such things as right from wrong, true from false, and appropriate from inappropriate behavior. A six-year-old will lie or steal just to see if he or she can get away with it.

The final stage of cycle one is a time of drawing conclusions. Ten-year-olds are quite secure in their perceptions and opinions about everything, having organized their lives in an orderly and systematic way. These children have the world figured out.

Then puberty comes along and wipes out the whole thing. The blackboard is erased, and the cycle essentially repeats itself. As adulthood looms large in front of young adolescents, they once again go through a time of discovery. Young adolescents are notorious for exploring and experiencing everything, trying things on for size just like a little child. If you have ever noticed similarities between middle schoolers and toddlers, this may partially explain it. Middle schoolers are inquisitive and have a need to experience everything they possibly can. They are open to whatever the world has to offer them.

This time of discovery is followed once again by a time of testing and a time of concluding. But it is during young adolescents' middle-school years that they are most open to new ideas and new ways of thinking.

This openness often takes the form of gullibility or vulnerability. Middle schoolers are not always the most discriminating people in the world and will try almost anything once. That's why people who work with this age consider middle schoolers to be the most at risk. Whatever is going around has to be tried. Fads are big on middle-school campuses. These kids are easy targets for advertisers, rock-and-roll disc jockeys, drug pushers, and anyone selling just about anything. This age group is willing to try out new things and take risks that older teens and adults will think twice about. As one popular news magazine reported recently,

> Too old for Ronald McDonald, too young for the car keys. Yet today's 25 million "tweens" from 9 to 15 no longer are viewed by Madison Avenue as the $2 allowance crowd. More marketers are pitching products directly at youngsters. . . . To marketers, these impressionable and seemingly insatiable kids, who buy or influence the purchase of $45 billion worth of goods a year, represent not only a treasure trove but an opportunity to convert an entire generation to brands they might buy for life.[8]

We can't afford to play a passive role concerning what influences our children and captures their imaginations. We must pay attention to the kinds of things that our kids are being exposed to. We are not always in a good position to control what influences them or what they are exposed to, but we can talk to them about it and monitor what they are thinking.

Earlier we described the myth of the teenage werewolf. There is another myth that parents often believe—the one that says "parents have little or no influence on their children after they reach adolescence." The popular wisdom is that peers and the electronic media (TV, movies, music) have greater influence than parents. This is simply not true. Throughout early adolescence, parents remain in the best position to positively or negatively influence their kids.[9] We can't afford to abdicate this position either to peers or to the media. If we want our kids to develop positive values and to have a meaningful faith, then we need to be involved with our kids during this time when they are more open to new ideas than they will be at any other time in their lives. We need to provide our kids with the best input they can get.

A Time of Decision

A recent survey of more than eight thousand young adolescents revealed that the value that increases most between fifth grade and ninth grade is "to make my own decisions."[10] As middle schoolers approach adulthood, they covet this one characteristic of adulthood that has been withheld from them.

Parents, guardians, and other authority figures make the important decisions for children. But as they approach adolescence, kids want the right to begin making such decisions for themselves. This doesn't mean that middle schoolers want to be independent. Actually, they want autonomy, the ability to make a few decisions about things that are important to them. They want to decide who their friends will be, what clothes they will wear, and what music they will listen to. Likewise, they are anxious to make decisions about their values, faith, and other commitments. Their quest for autonomy pushes them to make as many of the decisions that govern their lives as possible.

I have always been amazed at how easy it is to get middle-school kids to "make decisions" at a church camp or youth meeting. That's why I have tried to be very careful not to manipulate them or push them into decisions that they may not be ready to make. On the other hand, the decisions they make are important and serve an important function.

Most people agree that middle schoolers don't make decisions that last very long. Some well-known adolescent psychologists have written that young adolescents are incapable of "installing lasting idols or ideals as guardians of a final identity."[11] Most middle schoolers are engaged in a fact-finding period that makes the majority of their assumptions, conclusions, and decisions fragile and temporary. But for some of them, significant decisions are possible, and these choices may have considerable impact upon our kids for the rest of their lives. I know many people who, when asked when they made their first commitment to Christ, point to their early adolescent years.

What can we say about such decisions? Simply that the decision-making process begins (or at least gains impetus) during early adolescence and that some of these decisions will receive enough confirmation and support in the years that follow to last.

Jeremy was a boy in my youth group who I think "accepted Christ as Savior" about thirty-five times. Theologians may have a problem with that fact, but as a youth worker and parent, I have no problem with it at all. Jeremy needed to make a decision for Christ thirty-five times. He is a fine Christian man today because the cumulative effect of "deciding for Christ" all those times made a big difference in his life.

I look at it this way: Middle schoolers have reached an important crossroad. They are no longer little children. They are ready to take some responsibility for their lives. They can make good decisions or bad decisions. If diagrammed, it might look like this:

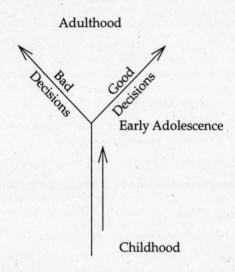

Adulthood

Bad Decisions   Good Decisions

Early Adolescence

Childhood

The diagram illustrates the road from childhood. When children reach adolescence (the Y in the road), they are faced with their first opportunity to make decisions on their own. On their journey to adulthood, they can choose to go down the road of bad decisions or the road of good decisions. The diagram emphasizes the road to the final destination, not the destination itself. Middle schoolers can set themselves on a course which is life shaping. Decisions made during early adolescence may not be final, but they are extremely significant and foundational to the rest of life. For this reason, their importance should never be underestimated.

Knowing this prompts the question, How can we help our kids make good decisions? We want our children to avoid making the kinds of decisions they will regret for the rest of their lives.

Obviously, there is no way we can prevent our kids from making a few bad choices. That is neither a reasonable nor a worthwhile goal. The best way to learn how to make wise decisions is to make a few unwise ones. We learn from our mistakes.

In his book, *Waiting*, Ben Patterson tells this story.

> I read of a young man who had just been appointed to the presidency of a bank at the tender age of thirty-two. The promotion was far beyond his wildest dreams and very frightening to him, so he went to the venerable old chairman of the board to ask for advice on how to be.
>
> "What is the most important thing for me to do as a new president?" he asked the older man.
>
> "Right decisions," was the gentleman's terse answer.
>
> The young man thought about that for a moment, and said, "Thank you very much; that is very helpful. But can you be a bit more specific? How do I make good decisions?"
>
> The wise old man answered, "Experience."
>
> Exasperated, the young president said, "But that is why I'm here. I don't have the experience I need to make right decisions. How do I get experience?"
>
> "Wrong decisions," came the old man's reply.[12]

Many young people fail to learn from their wrong decisions because they lack guidance. They are bound to repeat their bad choices. As parents, we need to help our kids process their mistakes by asking questions like, What happened? Why did it happen? What was the result? Was the outcome bad or good? What can be done differently next time to get a better result? If we can talk with our middle schoolers in a rational, helpful way, rather than scolding and reprimanding them, they will learn much more from their decisions and benefit from our experience.

One effective way to teach young adolescents how to

make good decisions is called role taking. Simply put, role taking is allowing your children to participate in the decisions that you make. When you make a purchase, for example, it helps middle schoolers to understand what was involved in making the decision. Many young people never realize what is involved in buying a big-ticket item such as a home or car. How do you decide which one to buy? How do you pay for it? How do you know whether or not you can afford it? These are important considerations, and many young people never consider them until they are young adults—when it's too late.

Take your kids shopping with you while they are young. Let them help you decide what to do when you have a big decision to make. Have a family meeting and decide together what you are going to do for your family vacation this summer. The only way our kids will learn how to make decisions is by making decisions. Give them every opportunity to do so when you can offer guidance and encouragement.

Helping middle schoolers learn to make good decisions is especially important in today's world because kids are faced with more options and choices than ever before. In the past, things were very clear—black and white, right and wrong, true and false. But today, everything is a shade of gray. We have moved from a true-false society to a multiple-choice society, and many of our kids are confused. They don't know what choices are valid or desirable. Many competing voices try to influence their decisions. Dr. Victor Stursburger, of the American Academy of Pediatrics, has written:

> These are the most dangerous times adolescents have ever had to face. There are more choices teens have to make at younger ages and less guidance to make those choices. Now, 14- and 15-year-olds are having to decide, "Am I going to have sex or not?" "Am I going to do drugs or not?" "Am I going to drink beer or not?" Two generations ago those decisions were made in college. A generation ago, they were made in high school. Now they're being made in middle school.[13]

33

Yes, these are dangerous times, but they are also opportune times for parents to help their children grow into responsible, capable adults who are strong and healthy in their physical, intellectual, emotional, social, and spiritual lives. It is to these areas that we now turn.

CHAPTER 2

The Perils of Puberty

On the way home from church one Sunday, Lisa's mom noticed a foul odor in the car. Lisa was only eleven years old, but it was obvious that her body chemistry was beginning to change.

"Lisa, I think the time has come for you to start wearing deodorant," her mother announced, expecting this bit of news to be welcomed with the usual range of moans and protests. Instead, Lisa broke into a wide grin and yelled, "Hooray!"

Normally people don't cheer for body odor, but in the case of an eleven-year-old girl, body odor is something to celebrate. It's a sure sign that she is growing up—that she is becoming a woman. It is a rite of passage into adulthood.

That rite of passage is called puberty and, next to birth itself, it is the most drastic physical change that we experience.[1] Unlike birth, however, puberty is a change that we are aware of and get to watch. For the middle schoolers who are doing the watching, not all that they see is worth celebrating. Puberty can be distressing and anxiety producing.

In this chapter, we will take a close look at what happens to a typical middle schooler's body. Young adolescents are going through enormous physical changes. That's why it's so tough to keep them in the same clothes for more than a few months. They outgrow them very rapidly. Fortunately, this change only happens once in a person's lifetime—

during the middle-school years. That's when our children are physically transformed into adults.

Puberty Strikes

At what age does puberty usually occur?

In the United States, the average age for menarche (when a girl has her first menstrual period) is 12.9 years. That event is usually considered the milestone for measuring when puberty occurs for girls. The female adolescent growth spurt actually begins much earlier—at about 9.6 years. Its peak velocity is at about age 11.8. Comparable milestones occur almost two years later for boys.[2] (The event that parallels menarche for boys, by the way, is generally considered to be the first ejaculation or wet dream.)

This is why girls are usually bigger than boys during early adolescence and are more fully developed. The boys don't catch up with the girls physically until about age fifteen. This delay creates some awkward problems in communication and relationships between boys and girls. When boys are starting to show an interest in girls, they discover that the girls are interested in older boys.

Keep in mind that while the above figures are fairly accurate, they are not absolute. There is a wide range in the normal onset and duration of puberty. It is not unusual for two boys who are the same age to be as much as four years apart in physical development during early adolescence. It is well within normal range for boys to experience the onset of puberty anywhere between the ages of ten and fourteen, give or take another year or two. Add to that the fact that girls can be two years ahead of boys developmentally, and you have the possibility that two middle schoolers, a boy and girl who are the same age, may be six years apart in terms of physical development. A great difference exists between a fast-developing girl and a slow-developing boy, but both of them are normal.

The average age for the onset of puberty is lower today

than it was a hundred years ago. Studies in the United States have shown that in the year 1900, the average age of menarche was 14.2 years, compared with today's 12.9.[3] In other countries, the downward trend has been even more severe as the population has become more "civilized."

Coinciding with this earlier maturation has come an increase in height and weight. This has led many experts to think that modern society's eating habits—better nutrition, more protein and calories—have been a major contributor to earlier puberty. Bigger people seem to experience puberty earlier. (History records that some parents have actually tried to starve their kids to keep them from growing up too fast.)

No one knows the exact reason for earlier maturation. Likewise, no one knows whether this trend will continue, although recent evidence suggests that things have stabilized considerably over the last twenty-five years.[4] Let's hope so. Otherwise, we might see the day when kids go through puberty before they enter kindergarten!

Regardless of when puberty happens, the bottom line is that middle-school children are in the process of becoming adults. It is unfortunate that in our culture this very important and significant event in the life of a young person is hardly acknowledged. When recognized, puberty is often viewed in a negative context. Sometimes it is regarded as a disease, a problem, an inconvenience. Lisa's mother wasn't pleased that her daughter had begun stinking up her clothes.

Some past cultures (and some cultures today) celebrated puberty with more ritual than merely distributing a can of deodorant. Among some Native American tribes, when a boy or girl manifested the physical signs of adulthood (menarche, pubic hair), the tribe would conduct ceremonial rites of passage to memorialize and sanctify one's passage from childhood into adulthood. The transition would be a matter of public record. For girls, these rites often included a celebration of the first menstruation, formal training in sexual matters, and instruction in domestic arts such as cooking and making clothes.

Boys, not having such a well-defined and observable event as menarche to signal their passage from childhood to adulthood, would sometimes be taken off in the company of the men, tutored in the duties and privileges of manhood, and allowed to emerge officially as a man. Among some Native American tribes, a boy would go out alone on a vision quest. He would return, reborn, with a new name—his name as a man.

This passage from childhood to adulthood is not nearly so well-defined or brief in our society. We ask our middle schoolers, who are clearly emerging adults, to wait another eight or ten years before claiming their adulthood. Some young people don't think of themselves as adults even after they turn eighteen or twenty-one.

Perhaps the only rite of passage for the average teenager is obtaining a drivers' license. For most teens, getting their license is a highly significant event that symbolizes their adult status.

Other than that, kids have no way of gaining a clear vision of who they are and what their role is in society or the family. In the past, when rites of passage were definite and clear, young people knew exactly where they stood. Yesterday, they were children and were treated as children. But tomorrow, they will become adults and will be treated like adults.

When young adolescents are unsure whether they are children or adults, they act accordingly. They try to pick up signals from their parents and other adults. "How am I treated? Am I treated like a child? . . . Then I must be a child. Am I treated with dignity and respect? Do people take me seriously? . . . Then I must be an adult."

Wise parents create a few meaningful rites of passage for their children as they make their journey from childhood to adulthood. Psychologist David Elkind calls such rites markers.

We all have a "sense of becoming," of growing and changing as individuals. Markers confirm us in our sense of growing and changing. This confirmation, moreover, has to be social as well as personal. However personally gratifying the attainment of certain markers is, such attainments mean much more when accompanied by social recognition. Indeed, much of the gratification of reaching new markers is the public approval that comes with them. Confirmation, bar or bas mitzvah, graduation exercises, and the like provide a public acknowledgment that young people have attained new levels of maturity. Public recognition confirms teenagers in their sense of progress and growth.[5]

It is not necessary to re-institute ancient rites of passage such as vision quests and menstrual celebrations, but we can acknowledge in concrete ways that our kids are growing up. When my daughter experienced her first period, I simply bought a small bouquet of roses which I placed in her bedroom. She was pleased that I considered this event to be significant. I wanted her to know that in my eyes she was no longer a child. She had become a young woman, and I would from now on treat her as such.

What's Happening

Middle schoolers' bodies change in many ways during puberty, and these changes are accompanied by an equal number of puzzling new experiences—some exciting, some embarrassing, and others just plain awful. When these "perils of puberty" occur, it's hard for many young adolescents to understand them or adjust to them. What makes it even worse is that no one else talks much about them, and those who do are often misinformed.

For girls, the most noticeable of these changes are a general acceleration in both height and weight, a widening of the hips, and the appearance of breasts. At this age, girls become softer, rounder, and grow very concerned about their figures. They want to look good in a bathing suit, and they want boys to notice them.

This can be a very frustrating time for girls who are concerned that they are growing too much or too little in the wrong places and who insist upon comparing themselves with their friends or with the girls they see in fashion magazines. Breasts have become such a preoccupation in our society that girls with small breasts often fear boys will never like them. Girls worry, too, if one breast grows faster than the other, which is not unusual. Dr. Maryanne Collins, pediatrician and specialist in adolescent medicine, wrote, "When a young girl starts to develop breasts, one side always enlarges first. Invariably mothers and daughters get concerned because they do not realize that this is normal."[6]

Girls also worry if their breasts enlarge too quickly. A girl with "too much" is often the object of ridicule from other girls and of some unpleasant joking from the boys. Breast-reduction surgery has become a fad in recent years, and many teenage girls consider it. Most girls could benefit from some assurance that beauty and sex appeal is rarely dependent on the breasts or any other part of the body. Breasts, like women, come in all shapes and sizes.

Girls usually experience their first period during their middle-school years. This can be a real shock if they aren't prepared for it. Accidents occur at the worst times and can be very embarrassing. Menstruation for young girls is frequently accompanied by abdominal pains, lack of energy, and irritability. Also, it takes a while before most girls have their period on a regular cycle. They might go three months without having a period and then have two very close together. This can cause a lot of worry. If it happens to your daughter, assure her that it is normal.

The first frustration boys experience with puberty is that they don't develop as early as the girls do. But when boys experience the onset of puberty, they grow rapidly and unevenly. It is not uncommon for boys to grow as much as six inches in one year, yet the arms, legs, and trunk may grow disproportionately and result in awkwardness and clumsiness. Just when a boy is becoming more coordinated, puberty strikes, and his progress is set back. Some boys worry that they are going to be too short because they aren't growing fast enough.

Appetites increase dramatically at this age as well. Most young adolescent boys can easily out-eat adults. Your grocery bill will undoubtedly reflect this.

Another noticeable change is the deepening voice, creating embarrassing moments when it changes pitch in the middle of a sentence. Acne is another peril of puberty that is common to both boys and girls.

Perhaps the most telltale sign of approaching manhood is the emergence of pubic hair. For boys, pubic hair is similar in significance to breasts for girls. Until you grow a crop of pubic hair around the genitals, your manhood remains seriously in doubt. Taking a shower after a Phys. Ed. class can be a traumatic experience for a slow developer. Visit a boys' locker room at a middle school, and you will usually find a shower area that hasn't had water hit the floor in weeks. When I was directing summer camps for this age group, it was typical for boys not to change their underwear all week long. Better to wear a little dirty underwear than to be embarrassed by being seen naked.

A boy's first ejaculation usually occurs while he is asleep, hence the term "wet dream." Unprepared boys may think they have wet the bed (more worry and guilt). Other worries include the size of one's penis (in comparison with others that they have seen or heard about) and spontaneous erections (occurring at the most inappropriate times). Experimental masturbation is also common with this age group.

One noticeable result of all this changing and growing—for both boys and girls—is a baffling schedule of energy bursts and apparent laziness. There are times when middle schoolers seem ready to explode with energy, and other times when they seem like the laziest creatures on earth.

Thirteen-year-old Aaron would come home from school, plop down in front of the television set, and sit with a blank look on his face. He would only move to get food. His parents (who were workaholics) were worried and frustrated by Aaron's sedentary behavior. They constantly urged him to "do something constructive." Do homework, mow the lawn, or at least go outside and get involved in some fun activity with the other kids. But Aaron always resisted, and the result was a lot of arguing and conflict.

Aaron's parents needed to know that Aaron's behavior is typical of boys this age. What Aaron really needed to do when he came home from school was take a nap. He was wiped out from all the growing and changing his body was doing. If you were growing that fast, you'd be tired, too.

So it is with most young adolescents. There are a lot of changes going on, and most of them are uneven, unpredictable, unexpected, and misunderstood. We need to be patient with our kids, empathize, and help them realize that what is happening to them is normal and good. They are growing up. That's something to celebrate.

PHYSICAL CHANGES DURING ADOLESCENCE

Boys
Development of penis and testicles
Pubic hair growth
Involuntary ejaculation
Enlargement of neck
Broadening of shoulders
Growth of armpit hair
Marked growth of hair on face and body
Deepening of voice
Increase in activity of sweat glands
Growth spurt in height and weight
Growth of muscle tissue

Girls
Development of ovaries and uterus
Pubic hair growth
Onset of menstruation
Breast development
Widening of hips
Growth of armpit hair

Slight growth of hair on face and body
Slight deepening of voice
Increase in activity of sweat glands
Growth spurt in height and weight
Growth of fat-bearing cells

Look at Me

When Jonathan was younger, he reminded everyone of Rodney Dangerfield. His clothes looked like they had been slept in (they had), his shirt-tail hung out, his shoelaces were left untied, his zipper was open, his hair was a mess, and yellow chunks of "sleep" were in his eyes. "Jon, get back in here and clean up! You look like a slob!" his parents would shout as he headed out the door for school.

But when Jonathan became a middle schooler, things changed. He started carrying a hairbrush. He grew concerned about the appearance of his clothes, especially the labels on them. He began getting up an hour early so he would have time to get ready for school. He took excruciatingly long showers (leaving little hot water in the house for anyone else). He started worrying about his pimples, his height, his weight, his hair, his ears, his muscles. In short, Jonathan became obsessive about his looks.

Jonathan is typical of young adolescents. They suddenly develop a new awareness of their bodies. Mirrors serve overtime duty during these years, and kids become very concerned with their appearance—whether they are good-looking or attractive and whether they measure up to others their age. They are, in their own secret fears, growing too rapidly, too slowly, too unevenly, or developing too much in all the wrong places. And for many, these fears are justified. Physical growth can be very uneven during early adolescence and become a source of great anxiety and grief.

Recent studies have confirmed that worry "about my looks" peaks in the eighth grade: 69 percent of girls and 49 percent of boys in that grade list this as their main worry.[7]

We adults worry about the economy or about how we are ever going to get things done. But young adolescents worry about the size of their noses.

One middle-school girl described herself this way.

> Every day, just about, something new seems to be happening to this body of mine and I get scared sometimes. I'll wake up in the middle of the night and I can't go back to sleep, and I toss and I turn and I can't stop my mind; it's racing fast, and everything is coming into it, and I think of my two best friends and how their faces are all broken out, and I worry mine will break out, too, but so far it hasn't, and I think of my sizes, and I can't get it out of my head—the chest size and the stomach size and what I'll be wearing and whether I'll be able to fit into this kind of dress or the latest swimsuit. Well, it goes on and on, and I'm dizzy, even though it's maybe one o'clock in the morning, and there I am, in bed, so how can you be dizzy?
>
> Everything is growing and changing. I can see my mother watching me. I can see everyone watching me. There are times I think I see people watching me when they really couldn't care less! My dad makes a point of not staring, but he catches his look, I guess. I'm going to be "big-chested"; that's how my mother describes herself! I have to figure out how to dress so I feel better—I mean, so I don't feel strange, with my bosom just sticking out at everyone! I have to decide if I should shave my legs! I will! . . . I wish a lot of the time I could just go back to being a little girl, without all these problems and these decisions![8]

This young lady describes vividly how many middle schoolers feel. They worry tremendously about their appearance and about how their bodies will turn out when they stop growing. Ordinarily, it's not a neurotic kind of worrying. Most kids don't lose sleep over their pimples, although some do. And though there are actual cases on record of young people who have committed suicide (or attempted it) because they perceived themselves as being ugly, such cases are extreme.

Usually this worry is a hidden fear that affects the lives of young people in ways they are not aware of at the time. The slow developer who feels inadequate or out of place may try to compensate by becoming withdrawn or unusually boisterous. Many middle schoolers will require a great deal more privacy than before. They will lock themselves in the bathroom for long periods of time while they examine themselves or try to improve their appearance.

Privacy is a very important issue to young adolescents. At church camps for this age group, I have watched kids hang towels and blankets all around the bunk beds in their cabins to have private places to change clothes. Such behavior is not unusual or unreasonable. I visited a junior high school a few years ago and was shocked to discover that in the bathrooms the doors were missing from all the toilet stalls. I discovered later that the school authorities had removed the doors because they suspected that the kids were smoking cigarettes and dealing drugs inside the stalls. They believed that removing the doors would prevent such behavior. Unfortunately, what it prevented was not smoking and drug dealing, but using the toilet. They ended up with a school full of constipated kids.

Nobody Likes Me

The main reason young adolescents are obsessed with their appearance and their physical development is that it dramatically affects their social lives. In their view, if they don't look good, nobody will like them. And being liked is a very important issue for middle schoolers.

Little children are able to make instant friends with anyone their age. It is always fun to watch them on the playground, playing with each other regardless of race, creed, color, looks, or gender. But as children reach the age of puberty, their innocence fades. They become much more selective in their associations. Suddenly there are those who are popular or cool and those who are unpopular or nerds. Popular kids don't have much to do with unpopular kids, and vice versa. This extremely rigid caste system lasts for years and is particularly noticeable during middle school. To be unpopular is terrible in the eyes of most kids, and of course, it's everyone's dream to be counted among the popular elite.

What is it that makes a person popular or unpopular? Most of the time it will have something to do with physical characteristics, such as how a person looks or how well developed an individual is. Early developing boys who are athletic, tall, and good-looking tend to be most popular. Girls who are pretty and have attractive figures and nice hair are likely to be popular. Kids who are ugly (or plain), short, fat, or "flat" are doomed. Unfortunately, this is made even worse by our culture's overemphasis on being beautiful and sexy (as seen on TV and in magazines). Young adolescents (and most adults) place great value on physical characteristics. It's a matter of social survival.

Judy Blume's book *Letters to Judy* includes a number of revealing letters that the author has received from young people who are unhappy with their bodies. The following letter from a twelve-year-old girl is typical:

> Dear Judy,
>   Hi, my name is Emily. I am twelve years old and live in Kansas. In fifth grade I had a lot of boyfriends, but now I am in seventh grade and I have none. It is because I am flat. All the boys tease me and call me "Board." Sometimes I feel like crying. All my friends talk about their periods and about shaving. I am afraid to ask my mother for a razor or a bra or a deodorant. One day I took my brother's deodorant so I would have some for gym.[9]

A middle-school girl may become preoccupied with her appearance because she is convinced that her entire future depends on it. She may believe that if she isn't attractive, she won't be popular, won't have dates, won't get married, won't be able to get a job, and won't have children. Her life is over! This view of the future, distorted as it may be, leaves some girls depressed and despairing. Other girls embark on a strenuous program to repair their supposed defects with cosmetics, exercises, diets, and an endless quest for that miracle product that will make them look like one of their supermodel heroines. Tragically, some young adolescent girls develop serious eating disorders (anorexia and bulimia) because they are afraid of gaining weight.

In surveys and interviews that I have conducted with this age group, nearly all middle schoolers list as their heroes the most glamorous people in show business and sports. Their favorite television programs are those featuring heroic, beautiful, sexy, almost superhuman characters who are always successful and, more importantly, well-liked and admired by everyone. Every middle schooler fantasizes about being such a person. In response to the question, If you could change anything about yourself, what would it be? kids invariably list physical improvements—a new nose, new hair, new face, new shape, or a whole new body. Rarely do other qualities (such as intelligence or kindness) enter their minds.

Sometimes parents only make matters worse by overemphasizing physical appearance and encouraging kids to try to look like fashion models or to perform like sports heroes. Wise parents don't put additional pressure on their children in the area of physical development. Kids are rarely helped by constantly being harped at about physical defects and inadequacies, such as weight or coordination. Be careful about pushing young teens into sports and athletic competitions, especially if they are not enthusiastic about these activities. Protect your kids from needless put-downs, ridicule, and other embarrassing situations that call attention to their physical development.

I can relate to young adolescents who are struggling with how they look because I was a slow developer at their age and not as athletic as other boys. I hated Phys. Ed. classes at school. I enjoyed playing games and competing as much as the other boys, but I loathed those times when we had to choose up teams. I was inevitably chosen last and felt humiliated every time it happened, even though I didn't

47

blame anyone for not choosing me first. I was called a klutz, a label which stuck for several years. Eventually, I caught up with most of my classmates, but those early years were difficult. Slow developers have a significant disadvantage.

I visited a middle school recently and watched a seventh-grade volleyball game. What a disaster! The kids hated it and couldn't wait for the period to be over because most of them were unable to return the ball over the net successfully. I was tempted to step in and take over the class and show them a few games that were both fun and easy to play. There are plenty of very physical, athletic activities that middle schoolers can participate in and enjoy without being embarrassed.

Affirmation Is Where You Find It

When I was in ninth grade, I was arrested for shoplifting. My best friend and I were caught trying to walk out of a store, our coats lined with merchandise. That ended my career as a big-time thief.

Like most adolescent shoplifters, my friend and I didn't need anything we took. We usually gave most of it away to our friends. It was an exciting game, a challenge, and in retrospect, it was a way for us to prove our manhood. We hadn't been able to prove it any other way. We had tried out for the freshman football and baseball teams and failed. We weren't very popular. So we needed a way to show that we were courageous, adventurous, tough guys, and for a while, shoplifting was our answer. It made us look big in the eyes of our peers.

This kind of thinking is not uncommon among young adolescents who are slow developers or who have deep feelings of inferiority. The drive to be accepted by peers is strong and may cause these kids to compensate for their lack of physical prowess in undesirable or self-destructive ways. Smoking, drinking, drug abuse, sexual promiscuity, rowdy behavior, vandalism, foul language, fighting, joining gangs, running away from home, and breaking the law are only a few manifestations of this problem.

Kids can get the peer acceptance, ego satisfaction, and affirmation they need through positive and constructive means. After my "life of crime" in ninth grade, I became interested in graphic arts—drawing cartoons, designing posters, and painting signs. Soon this became my "thing." Everyone would come to me for artwork, and gradually those feelings of inferiority diminished. I felt proud that the most popular kids in school would ask me to help them with their publicity for school activities or for their student-body election campaigns.

Parents can help their children excel. In the past, this happened naturally because children made contributions to the family farm or the family business. They had no doubt that they were needed and valued by the family and the community. But in today's urban, industrialized society, kids are often viewed as liabilities rather than assets. As Elkind has written, today's youth have no place in today's society.[10]

Give your kids opportunities to succeed and affirm them whenever you can. Catch them in the act of doing something good. Notice when they accomplish a task that they set out to do. Compliment them when they say the right thing or handle a situation well. Don't attempt to flatter them or pump them up, but give them genuine opportunities to receive praise.

One of my fondest memories of my father is hearing him laugh at my jokes. My jokes weren't that funny, but I remember my dad practically falling on the floor with laughter. His affirmation did a lot to encourage my sense of humor and my performing instinct. He helped me believe that I was funny and entertaining, and that belief helped me accomplish things that wouldn't have been possible other-wise.

Sex and the Young Adolescent

I was the speaker at a weekend denominational youth conference for middle schoolers a few months ago when an amazing crisis took place.

On Saturday afternoon, an eighth grade girl named Heather was complaining of severe abdominal pain and vaginal bleeding. She was hysterical, and no one knew what was wrong with her. The pains persisted, and she was rushed to a hospital emergency room. An hour later, she gave birth to a baby girl.

The amazing thing was that Heather did not know she was pregnant.

It should come as no surprise that many middle-school kids are sexually active. The onset of puberty brings a heightened interest in sexual matters. Many kids become involved in some form of sexual activity—be it holding hands, looking at sexually explicit photographs, heavy petting, or sexual intercourse.

A 1984 study of some eight thousand young adolescents from a variety of church youth groups revealed that 16 percent of sixth graders, 15 percent of seventh graders, and 17 percent of eighth graders answered yes to the question, Have you ever had sexual intercourse ("gone all the way" or "made love")?[11] A more recent study found that 23 percent of all teenagers report that they were "under fourteen years old" when they had sex for the first time.[12]

While statistics like these may shock or alarm us, it is important to remember that today's young adolescents are not that different from adolescents of a generation or two ago. In 1954, William Carlos Williams wrote, "These kids get to be twelve or thirteen and they explode. They'll tell you that—energy is pushing through them, and some say they're going to ride with it, enjoy it, and not worry!"[13] Sexual feelings and desires during early adolescence are not new. It's a normal part of growing up.

What is new is that today's young people are living in a different kind of world. In spite of fears about AIDS and other sexually transmitted diseases, the overemphasis on sex in movies, television, popular music, and advertising encourages kids to engage in sexual activity much earlier. The message they seem to be getting is, Have sex now or die!

Because of the different rates at which kids develop, some teens will take an earlier interest in sex than others. It is never safe to assume that just because your middle schoolers don't talk about sex or about having a boyfriend or girlfriend, they are not interested in sex. Many children who have not reached puberty experiment with sex because of their early and continual exposure to it. Boys as young as six or seven years old will look at pornographic pictures and "talk dirty," pretending to know what they are seeing and talking about, or pretending to be interested simply because they think it is expected of them. Psychologists and social workers call this "social puberty."

It is wise to assume that middle-school children are old enough to be keenly interested in what sex is all about. They may not understand it all, and they may not be physically mature, but they are definitely interested.

Talking with Middle Schoolers About Sex

When I was a youngster, I assumed that my sexuality was sinful, or at least undesirable, simply because nobody ever talked about it. It was never brought up at home or at church or at school, and I, for one, was afraid to ask about it. Since my parents were Christians, I figured they probably wouldn't want to talk about it either. About the only sex education I got when I was young was the message that sex is dirty, filthy, and nasty, and that it should be saved for the one you marry.

The story is told of a boy whose homework assignment was to ask one of his parents where babies came from, and then write a report on the subject.

"Mom, where did I come from?" the boy asked.

"Well, um, the stork brought you," answered his mother.

51

"How about you. Where did you come from?"

"The stork brought me, too."

"And Grandma?"

"Same as you and me. The stork brought Grandma."

The boy went to his room and began writing his report: "There hasn't been a normal birth in our family in at least three generations. . . ."

While few parents resort to stories about storks and cabbage patches these days, things haven't changed much in the last thirty years. Kids are still not getting the straight scoop on sex, even though public schools have tried to pick up much of the slack in that area. Most schools now offer some kind of sex education in their curriculum. But because they often approach the subject in a value-free manner and treat it like an academic subject, they not only fail to answer the most important questions kids have about sex, but they also make the subject boring. One fourteen-year-old boy described his sex education class at school this way: "All these dumb little books. . . . I don't think they could teach me anything. Maybe how many sperm are in a drop of semen, but I don't even want to know that. It's not going to help me any."[14]

If you have a difficult time talking with your kids about sex, you are not alone. Most parents avoid the subject, even though they express a desire to teach their children about sex. One study found that although most parents of middle schoolers believe that sex education belongs in the home, only one-third of them actually do it.[15] Another study found that 45 percent of America's teenagers say they learn nothing from their parents about sex. "Three out of four say it's hard to talk to their fathers, and 57 percent find their mothers tough going. Only about a third (36%) say they would ask their parents for any desired sexual information, while almost half (47%) would turn to friends, sex partners, or siblings."[16] The following paragraph, written by a twelve-year-old girl, is typical:

My mother decided to finally have the talk with me. But I knew about that subject long before my mother told me about it. When she was telling me, she kept asking me if I had ever heard anything about that. I kept saying no, as if I had never heard a word. But you know how it is, everyone picks everything up on the streets. My mother wasn't the first one to tell me. Actually, she was the last.[17]

The truth of the matter is that most kids aren't learning all they need to know on the streets. In our age of "enlightenment," many young adolescents remain essentially uninformed and disturbingly ignorant concerning their sexuality and how their bodies are changing. It seems incredible that Heather, the middle-school girl who had a baby at a youth conference, didn't know she was pregnant. But it's true. Many young adolescents are ignorant of basic information about sex and its consequences.

You may get the impression from your middle schoolers that they know everything there is to know about sex. When you broach the subject, they will say, in effect, "I know that already" or "You can't tell me anything I don't already know." Don't let that keep you from talking with your kids about sex. Middle schoolers often act like they know everything because they don't want to admit their ignorance. You can be sure that they are insatiably curious and want to know more. They want to know the truth. Where are they going to get it?

Don't abdicate your responsibility for teaching your kids about sexual values. You can't assume that the schools or the media are providing adequate instruction and information about sex for your kids. Schools are increasingly shying away from teaching values about sex, simply because they are so controversial. Most public schools limit their instruction to the physiology of sex and instruct youth on the value of practicing "safe sex."

The media also teach our children about sex—simply because sex attracts viewers, especially young ones. But what values are the media teaching our children? One study found that the average viewer of prime-time television in

America will watch over nine thousand scenes depicting sexual intercourse or discussions of sexual intercourse in one year—and of those nine thousand scenes, less than 10 percent will involve married couples.[18] It is doubtful that you want your children to live by what the media teach them about sexuality.

Some parents erroneously think that if they don't bring up the subject, then their kids won't be concerned about it. They argue that talking about sex will only make kids more curious or overstimulate them and encourage experimentation. It doesn't work that way. Experimentation is caused by a lack of information, not an abundance of it. Ignoring the subject doesn't make it go away. Sooner or later (and it is usually sooner) kids will want information about their bodies, and if they don't get it at home, they'll get it somewhere else.

You may think that because your parents never talked to you about sex and you were still able to figure it out, your children won't need information from you. This may or may not be true—but today's young people are growing up in a vastly different world from the one we grew up in. A generation or two ago, the need for parents to instruct their children about sexual values was not as great as it is today. We may have survived with little or no help from our parents concerning sexual issues, but we mustn't use that as a rationalization for our own unwillingness to talk openly with our kids about the subject. "The Good Old Days" are long gone.

I realize that sex is still a taboo subject for family discussions, but it may be time to break the taboo before it breaks your family. Teach your children what you believe about sex. They want to know what you think—or if you think about it at all. (Some middle schoolers really do wonder where they came from. They can't imagine their parents ever having had sex.)

Share with them your values, convictions, and moral standards. Talk about dating, petting, premarital sex, marriage, and the family. Ask your kids how they feel about their bodies, about themselves, and about love. Use examples from your own youth. Discuss with your kids how you felt when you fell in love, started dating, and got married. You don't have to tell them everything you did, but they need to know that you understand what they are feeling and struggling with.

One way to talk with kids about sex indirectly is to talk over television. If you are watching television with your kids, there will be plenty of opportunities to comment on the sexual innuendo and situations that are portrayed. Don't turn the TV off or change channels when a suggestive situation comes up. Express your thoughts without being overly judgmental and prudish. Teach your kids to evaluate what they see based on biblical values which you and your family hold dear. Discussions teach kids how to think.

Ask questions of your kids, especially if they are having a hard time sharing problems with you. Use TV and other opportunities to introduce topics. Don't ask your kids personal questions of a sexual nature, but ask their opinions on general topics such as love, relationships, dating, birth control, AIDS, homosexuality, and pornography.

Sometimes your kids will have a difficult time expressing their opinions; that's okay. Don't give up. Keep asking those questions lovingly and gently. It lets kids know that you are interested and concerned. It also lets them know that you are willing to talk about anything. If you avoid bringing up tough topics like sex, your kids are learning that you are not approachable on those subjects. If they ever need someone to talk to, they most likely will go somewhere else. You want your kids to know that nothing is off-limits with you.

Middle-School Myths About Sex

Besides dealing with the basic issues of puberty, one of the first steps in teaching sex to middle schoolers is to help them unlearn some of the myths that they have picked up about sex from the media and other sources. It is amazing how much bad information kids have learned by the time they are ten or eleven years old. Here are just a few of those myths.

1. Sex is a big problem. Many kids believe this is true because they hear so much about the problems sex brings. Many TV shows are about problem love affairs or people getting venereal disease or AIDS from sex. They see all the how-to books and magazines and read the advice columns on how to overcome sexual dysfunction. Ads on the radio offer help for male impotence. Radio sex therapists discuss everyone's problems, no matter how bizarre they might be. Middle schoolers would benefit from the knowledge that despite what they hear in the media, sex is not a huge problem or a source of stress and anxiety for everyone. They need to know that many people have well-adjusted, enduring, satisfying, and yes, exciting sexual relationships within the bonds of marriage.

2. Sex is technique. Many young people believe from the books and magazines they read (as well as from sex education classes in school) that sex is ninety-nine percent technique, or "doing it." They need to know that making love involves much more than learning the mechanics of sex. It involves the whole person—mind, body, and soul. It is a relationship that requires time and commitment.

3. Everyone is doing it. Kids themselves like to perpetuate this common myth. It puts a lot of pressure on young people who have not become sexually active because they feel left out. The truth is that everyone is not doing it. There are millions of teenagers all over this country who have made sexual abstinence until marriage a lifestyle choice. We need to help our kids understand that "it's okay to say 'no way.'"

4. Sex makes the world go round. Due largely to over-exposure (literally) in the entertainment media, young people not only believe that sex must be the best thing there is, but that it's the only thing there is. We need to help our kids keep sex in its proper perspective.

5. *You prove your manhood* (or *womanhood*) *by having sex.*
Many young adolescents, especially boys, believe that sexual
prowess determines manhood. "Real men have sex a lot."
From what kids see in the movies and watch on TV, they
conclude that it is possible to have sex ten or twenty times a
day—and with different people each time! Of course, we
adults know that such behavior is not only unwise; it is
impossible.

It might be a good idea to remind our kids that the world-
champion copulators are not people, but rabbits and ham-
sters. Real men prove their manhood by accepting responsibility for their actions and demonstrating good judgment and
self-control.

Health Issues

Here's a joke that has been heard at some youth workers'
conferences: What's the difference between boogers and
broccoli? Answer: Middle schoolers don't eat broccoli.

There's some truth to that. Middle schoolers don't eat too
many green things or anything else that they think is good
for them. It's ironic that at the time adolescents are becoming
more aware of their bodies and more concerned about their
appearance and their physical development, they actually do
very little to take care of their bodies. Good health seems to
be a non-issue for them, perhaps because they think they are
invulnerable—that they will live forever. It's sometimes
quite difficult to help kids understand the importance of
proper nutrition and exercise.

It's no secret that young adolescents are notorious junk-
food junkies. Nutritionists are deeply concerned about the
long-range effects of the poor eating habits of today's youth.

The Maternal and Child Health Service reports that the
three groups most vulnerable to poor nutrition are infants
and young children, young adolescents, and expectant
mothers. Another survey on nutrition found that young
people between the ages of ten and sixteen had the highest

rates of unsatisfactory nutritional status, and boys more than girls. Problems included being underweight or undersize, obesity, iron-deficiency anemia, and dental decay. It is generally agreed that nutrition hits one of its all-time low points during adolescence.[19]

This is especially bad news when you consider that the adolescent growth spurt is second only to infant growth. The body, including the brain, is developing rapidly. There is strong evidence that malnutrition in infants directly affects intellectual competence, but little is known about how nutritional deficiencies affect the brain during later childhood and adolescence.

One thing we do know: A person's attitude toward physical health, like so many other values and beliefs, is formed early in life. The patterns that kids set for themselves during their middle-school years will be carried with them into later adolescence and adulthood.

I know it's difficult to persuade middle schoolers to eat properly and take care of their bodies, but we should do all we can to help our kids develop an awareness that our bodies are a gift from God and the "temple of the Holy Spirit" (1 Cor. 6:19). Your kids will moan and complain about having to eat their vegetables or having to do without their favorite junk food, but be persistent and do your "parental thing." Chances are good that someday they will thank you for caring.

CHAPTER 3
Making Friends

Jodie and Angela have been talking on the phone for over an hour about Denise and Rachel, who is Angela's best friend. Denise thinks she is Rachel's best friend, which may be true because Rachel has other best friends, including Megan. Of course, everybody wants to be Kim's best friend, because Kim is so popular. Jodie says it's because Kim is really friendly and doesn't have braces. Jodie hates to smile because when she smiles, her braces show and her gums look red and puffy, which explains why she's not as popular as Kim. Angela says she'd just die if Rachel and Kim became best friends. It's okay that Rachel has other best friends, but it wouldn't be okay if Kim were one of them because Kim likes Jeremy, the class hunk, who used to like Angela but now is going out with Denise.

Confused? This may sound a bit like something from *Days of Our Lives*, but it's actually a slice from a typical middle schooler's social life.

Young adolescents are developing socially in much the same way they are developing physically. A transition is going on. A new social awareness and social maturity is beginning to emerge. Relationships, especially with peers, become very important to middle schoolers. When these kids were younger, they only needed playmates, but now they need friends. There is a big difference between the two. Friends are people you can talk with, who can be trusted, who listen to you, and who understand your feelings.[1]

Loneliness becomes a terrible new experience for the young adolescent, and fear of rejection can become a source of anxiety and stress, often dictating behavior patterns and value choices. Middle schoolers will usually do whatever is most conducive to making friends and keeping them. Having friends is, quite simply, the lifeblood of adolescence.

Autonomy and Independence

Why the great need for friends at this age? To understand this, we must begin with a concept that shows up in practically all the literature on adolescent behavior. It is the quest for autonomy—the need for young adolescents to break ties with the family and to establish an identity that is separate from authority figures such as parents. Autonomy is another way of describing the young adolescent's need for independence.

As middle schoolers begin to make the transition from childhood to adulthood, they desire an identity of their own. They want to be their own person, to make their own choices and commitments, to be set free, to be treated like adults. This is the age when kids become highly critical of parents. They may consider you and your ideas to be hopelessly old-fashioned. They may be embarrassed by you and prefer not to be seen with you in public. They don't want to sit with you in church for fear that someone will mistake them for children. While there are exceptions to this kind of behavior, it is the norm for many young adolescents.

Delia Ephron, in her book *Teenage Romance*, offers this bit of parent-teen dialogue as an example:

> "Where are you going?"
> "Out."
> "Out where?"
> "Just out."
> "Who are you going with?"
> "A friend."
> "Which friend?"
> "Mom, just a friend, okay? Do you have to know everything?"

"I don't have to know everything. I just want to know who you're going out with."

"Debby, okay?"

"Do I know Debby?"

"She's just a friend, okay?"

"Well, where are you going?"

"Out."[2]

The Inevitability of Conflict

The separation that is taking place during early adolescence accounts for much of the conflict between parents and children at this age. Many parents are caught off guard by it. They find it hard to understand why they are suddenly losing control, why their children are becoming so "rebellious." They never had such problems before. *Is my child becoming the teenage werewolf I thought he would?* they wonder.

The answer is no. Certainly it is frustrating when your children, who were learning to be good, obedient boys and girls, seem to take a giant step backward. But remember that adolescent development often progresses via the "detour of regression." Things usually get worse (in terms of parental obedience and respect) before they get better. Parents who understand this will find parenting young adolescents a much less difficult experience.

Many parents, observing that their middle schoolers are trying to become independent, become more rigid and strict rather than encouraging such development in a healthy way. This inevitably results in conflict and strained parent-child relationships.

Who's in Control?

Conflict can be expected in two areas as children move toward adolescence. The first is in the area of power and control: Who makes the decisions in my life? As we discussed in chapter one, young adolescents have a strong desire to make their own decisions. As children, most (if not all) of their decisions were made by their parents. But as they journey toward adolescence, kids want to share in the power and make their own decisions. This often results in conflict with parents over such issues as choice of clothing, music, hairstyle, friends, entertainment, and extracurricular activities.

It's a good idea for parents to remember the old saying, "Give your kids some rope, but not enough to hang themselves." During early adolescence, children need to begin learning how to make their own decisions about matters that are important to them. They shouldn't be given power and control over every area of their lives, of course, but they should be allowed to make some choices.

It might be helpful to make a list such as the one below and decide at what ages you can give your children the right to make their own decisions in each area. One thing is certain: You can't wait until your kids are fully grown before you finally let them take responsibility for everything. Decisions should be apportioned out to youngsters a little at a time, especially during their middle-school years.

At What Age Will You
Allow Your Child to Decide ...

the music they listen to?
the friends they have?
the clothes they wear?
the movies they see?
what they do with their spare time?
the classes they take at school?
what they do with their money?
whether to attend church?
which TV shows to watch?
when or whom they date?
when to do homework?
whether to go to college?
the condition of their bedroom?

where they live?
whether to participate in family activities?

The thorny question, of course, is which decisions to allow your children and which decisions to keep for yourself. You need to prioritize decisions according to what is worth fighting over. There are some issues that you will want to retain strict control over and others that aren't worth the conflict. You need to decide what those are.

For instance, it is typical for middle schoolers to want to wear clothes or have a hairstyle that doesn't match your image of a well-dressed, well-groomed individual. What are you going to do? Is this a battle worth fighting? Are dress and hairstyle so morally significant that you cannot trust your children to make these decisions for themselves? Dress and hairstyle are probably more important to teenagers than to you. How they look is critically important to them. It affects their social standing and their ability to have friends. In most cases, it is best to trust our kids with a decision like this. It is more important to do what we can to affirm our kids and to keep them on our team.

Another area where conflict often occurs is behavior. Young teens want to behave in ways that prove their independence from their parents. They will often choose behavior that they know their parents dislike, simply to show that they are their own person and are capable of acting independently of parental control.

Sometimes behavioral autonomy takes the form of rebellion, but not always. Rebellion is a strong term and usually implies that the adolescent has created a tremendous amount of grief and suffering for the family. Not all adolescents rebel. It is better to assume that adolescents will *assert themselves* in some way. Sometimes it takes the form of rebellion, but most of the time it takes some milder form.

A good strategy for preventing serious, harmful rebellion is for parents to allow a certain amount of assertive behavior in areas that are not physically harmful or morally wrong. Again, your children may want to cut their hair a certain way or wear certain clothing or listen to certain music or be with their friends rather than going on a family activity. These preferences may be irritating or distressing to you, but unless you know for a fact that they are harmful or morally wrong, it might be best to allow your middle schoolers to participate in them. That doesn't mean you have to like them. I was thoroughly disgusted when my son got his ear pierced, but I allowed him to do it. So far as I could tell, it wasn't harmful or morally wrong. It was, after all, his ear—and his way of being different. It certainly was not something that I would do, and he knew it.

The Bridge to Independence

As we have seen, early adolescence is when children make their move toward adulthood and involves a relentless quest for autonomy or independence. This quest forms the long-term goal of adolescence. Kids want independence, but they don't necessarily want it this minute. They want it and fear it at the same time. There is a huge gap between the security of parental authority and the independence of adulthood. To charge out into the world on one's own is a pretty scary thing. Young adolescents will say that they want to be treated like adults and think for themselves, but down deep they lack the confidence (and competence) necessary to take on the responsibilities that go with it. Therefore, they need a middle ground, a "bridge"—something to make the transition from dependence (childhood) to independence (adulthood) less scary.

In today's society, the peer group (having friends) is the stepping stone or bridge that links dependence with independence. It is somewhat ironic that for middle schoolers to find their identity as individuals, they must first lose their identity in a group of friends. "It is a paradox of adolescence," observed Joan Lipsitz, "that it is possible to achieve this inner, apparently singular, sense of individuality only when one sees oneself in terms of a larger social context."[3]

That larger social context is the peer group. What the crowd does, the middle schooler does. <u>What the crowd likes, he or she likes. Such behavior appears to be the opposite of independent thinking.</u>

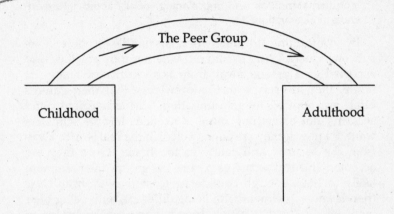

The need for this bridge accounts for the many fads so characteristic of the middle-school years as well as the inevitability of cliques and associations that often seem so negative. But this conformity, strange as it may seem, is an essential part of adolescent development and helps these kids gain the security and confidence needed for adulthood.

Educators Howard and Stoumbis described the situation this way:

> In his desire for independence, the young adolescent appears to become a rigid conformist to the mores, dress, speech, and attitudes of his fellows. Security is found in identifying with the group insofar as is at all possible. If group standards denigrate strong academic performance, the high grades are for "squares" and "goody-goodies." The seventh-grade pupil who was a strong student becomes only an average ninth-grade student, which confuses and shocks his parents and teachers. The young adolescent is almost certain to develop an air, a manner of sophistication or pseudo-sophistication, which he hopes will cover up the worries, doubts, and feelings of uncertainty that are

usually with him. During this time the young adolescent is highly susceptible to undesirable influences and individuals—if they are admired by his peer group. To gain status and recognition he must conform to these new standards. The role of the school should be obvious in developing desirable values, attitudes, standards, and in providing socially approved experiences and situations.[4]

By conforming to their friends, middle schoolers are subconsciously trying to find out whether they are liked and accepted as a person away from the security of home. At home, they are secure in the knowledge that their parents offer acceptance, love, admiration, encouragement, and security, but something more is needed. Middle schoolers want to know if they are equally okay in the real world, away from the security and safety of the home. Once they are accepted and feel secure as part of the group, they are more likely to have enough confidence to step away from their friends and experiment with being different, with being their own person. In that sense, friends serve as the bridge to independence.

A few years ago I conducted a survey of some seven hundred seventh and eighth graders from all over the United States. I asked each one of them to answer a number of questions. One of the questions was, If you could ask any question and get a straight answer, what would it be? Naturally, I received many different responses, but the most common answer was, "Do you like me?" These kids wanted to know if they were liked and accepted by others. They weren't concerned about the great theological issues of the day or how they could be better Christians at school or what the future holds. The real issue for most middle schoolers is, Am I okay? Do you like me?

More recent research has produced similar findings. One study found that "not being liked" ranks at the top of a long list of "worries" that young adolescents have.[5] Middle schoolers worry more about being liked than they do about anything else—including death. Being accepted by others is a matter of life and death to them, and they will more often than not pledge absolute loyalty to whoever will give them that acceptance. Teens who join gangs put their lives at great risk in order to be included in a group that accepts them and treats them with respect.

Of course, everyone wants to be liked, including you and me, but the special insecurities of early adolescence give this need a much greater significance. Our kids' need to be liked is linked closely with their emerging adulthood and their quest for independence. They are not certain whether they are likable, and they recognize that quality as an important prerequisite for acceptance as an adult in an adult world.

Do you remember how you pulled away from your parents during your early teens and tried to be your own person? I was very much like my parents, as most youngsters are, during my preteen years. My values, beliefs, and tastes were almost identical to those of my parents. I remember as a child listening to country music (and liking it!) because my mother and father did. I knew all the words to "Your Cheatin' Heart" and never missed the *Grand Ole Opry* program on television.

But along about the fourth or fifth grade, I realized that other kids my age did not listen to country music, and for the first time, that knowledge made an impact on me. Much to my parents' dismay, through junior high and high school, I listened to rock music. Country music was the music of my parents, and there was no way I was going to be caught dead listening to it. My father and I would fight for control of the radio whenever we got into the car. All the other kids liked rock and roll, and so did I. To not have liked it would have been incredibly foolish.

But as a senior in high school and during college, I finally dared to leave the security of the crowd. By that time I had the courage to strike out on my own and be a little different. I became a great fan of folk music, then bluegrass and country music. I learned to play a banjo. I came full circle, and for my parents it was like the return of the Prodigal Son.

That's the way it usually goes in early adolescence. It is

normal and necessary for middle schoolers to lose their identities in order to find them. Failure to conform (even when the group is doing something wrong) can produce feelings of guilt and inadequacy as severe as the feelings involved in going against one's conscience. Caught between a rock and a hard place, kids face a difficult struggle. This is what we usually mean by peer pressure. *Should I do what my friends want me to do, or should I do what I know is right?* young teens ask themselves. They know that either choice will lead to painful consequences.

Conformity to the peer group is not all bad. Of course, it is never all good, either. Middle schoolers are uniquely vulnerable; they can choose the wrong friends and get involved in things we do not approve of. But the alternatives are usually worse. Better a little bad influence than no friends at all. We can counter the bad influences that our kids are exposed to simply by keeping them on our team. We risk losing our kids when we don't permit them to have friends or we constantly put down their friends. A great many adults haven't yet grown up or are seriously maladjusted emotionally or psychologically simply because they were never able to fit in as adolescents. It is not uncommon to find adults still conforming to every whim of the crowd, hoping to find the acceptance they never received during their teen years.

Parents can offer guidance, but it is rarely helpful when they overreact to an important part of adolescent development. In the words of educator Jerome Kagan, "The early adolescent needs many peers to help him sculpt his beliefs, verify his new conclusions, test his new attitudes."[6] In Christian families, some parents use Scripture verses such as "Be not conformed . . . ," to tell their kids that they should only have "approved" friends. Romans 12:2 was not intended to be interpreted or used in that way. For good or bad, acceptance by and conformity to the peer group is a primary method children use to socialize themselves into adulthood.

It is important to remember that all children are different. Some need many friends; others need few. Some kids prefer to remain loners during much of their adolescence. There is nothing necessarily wrong with them. There may be a problem—with self-image, with relational skills, or with something that may be causing the child to be rejected by other kids—and if so, it should be addressed. But in most cases, kids who enjoy solitude or who aren't compelled to have lots of friends are simply kids who feel more comfortable being alone, staying close to parents, or—like the twelve-year-old Jesus—hanging out with elders in the temple. The norm is not always normal when applied to individuals. Everyone is different.

The Role of Adults

While the peer group serves an important function as the bridge to adulthood, it was not always this way. In earlier cultures, the adult community took the primary role in helping young people make their transition into adulthood.

The rites of passage described in chapter two are examples of how adult communities involved themselves in their children's transition into adulthood. Rites of passage were traditionally public events which acknowledged and permitted young people's entry into the adult world. From then on, adults in the community no longer regarded these young people as children—strictly under the care of their parents— but as young adults, ready to become part of the adult world. Adults gave these young people a place in society where they could learn the responsibilities of adulthood and receive a controlled introduction to adult life. In colonial America, for example, adolescents were given entry level jobs in the community. Boys were given apprenticeships from ages fourteen to twenty-one, girls from twelve to eighteen. Working alongside adults, they could learn a variety of trades, such as farmer, shipbuilder, barber, hatter, or baker.[7]

It is neither honest nor useful to romanticize the past— there can be no denying, for instance, that adolescents were often badly mistreated in colonial America. Still, it is clear that in the past, adults played a much larger role in the lives of adolescents than they do today. There have always been peer groups and peer friendships, but they have never before been as dominant in the development of adolescents.

In today's world, adolescents learn how to be adults primarily from each other. This is why the youth culture exists (a relatively recent phenomenon). It is a place where kids can practice being adults. They practice on each other. This mini-world has its own customs, styles, music, dress, and language. It is a middle ground between childhood and adulthood where kids can come to terms with who they are apart from their parents.

Why has this change taken place? Why is it that adults no longer involve themselves in the lives of teenagers? One obvious answer is that we don't live in the same kind of world. Rather than living in a rural, agrarian society like the one our ancestors knew, we live in an industrialized, technological society, which places many new demands and pressures on adults. The unfortunate result is that many adults have little time or energy to devote to their own kids, much less to other people's kids.

Psychologist David Elkind has written extensively about the negative impact these changes have on adolescents. In his book *All Grown Up and No Place to Go*, he wrote:

> In today's society we seem unable to accept the fact of adolescence, that there are young people in transition from childhood to adulthood who need adult guidance and direction. . . . In a rapidly changing society, when adults are struggling to adapt to a new social order, few adults are genuinely committed to helping teenagers attain a healthy adulthood. Young people are thus denied the special recognition and protection that society previously accorded their age group. . . . Young people today are quite literally all grown up with no place to go.[8]

Some people say that the crucial role of the peer group in the lives of young people is so universal that it must be considered one of the unchangeable laws of nature. And for quite a long time, I was convinced that God created the whole process.

I began to question this assumption after knowing several teens who had experienced rather serious problems trying to fit in with their peers. In one case, a boy with great potential had fallen in with the wrong crowd, committed a serious crime, and ended up in a juvenile detention facility to serve a ten-year sentence. In another case, a fourteen-year-old girl attempted suicide after she was rejected by some of her peers. If, as adolescent psychologists tell us, having friends is the natural, normal way for kids to make the transition from childhood to adulthood, why are so many problems associated with it? Why do so many bad things happen?

I don't believe psychologists and sociologists are wrong about the peer group's importance. It is vitally important. But this is true primarily because there is hardly any other way for young people to navigate the waters of adolescence safely. Young adolescents need someone other than their parents to whom they can turn for companionship, friendship, and guidance. They need other people to help them "sculpt their beliefs, verify their conclusions, and test their attitudes." The peer group is the one place where such a person is readily available.

Many, if not most, adolescents still seek out adults to fill that role. Unfortunately, it's not easy for kids to find adults who will come alongside them and treat them with dignity and respect. It's not easy to find adult friends. Most adults are busy being adults. They don't have time for kids.

The Myth of Peer Influence

As the parent of an adolescent, you will hear quite often that "the peer group has more influence on your child than anyone or anything else, including you." This is simply not true. Yes, the peer group does have influence, particularly when it comes to matters of dress, hairstyle, music, activities, and certain other behaviors. But when it comes to lasting influence—the kind that really matters—the only influence the peer group has comes *by default*. It is only influential in the absence of adults.

Studies have proven that throughout early adolescence, young people continue to look first to their parents for advice and guidance on important issues. Parents remain the primary models for their older adolescent children. While the influence of peers increases dramatically during early adolescence and the influence of parents decreases, the influence of peers never completely outweighs the influence of parents.[9] This is good news. We have influence over our kids, a fact we should never forget.

For years I have asked people, Who, beside your parents, had the greatest amount of influence on you when you were a teenager? The answer is always the name of an adult—a teacher, a coach, a neighbor, a relative, a pastor, a youth worker, an adult friend. No one ever mentions the name of a peer friend. Given that so many people believe that the peer group is number one in terms of influence over teenagers, this is a very interesting finding. Perhaps peers actually rank third in the "influence pecking order." While the peer group plays a vital role in the development of today's teenagers, kids still look to adults other than their parents for help and guidance, even though there are few adults willing to accept that role.

"Adolescents, left to their own devices, will always gravitate to the oldest person they can find who will take them seriously," said sociologist H. Stephen Glenn. This explains why young people are so vulnerable to celebrity worship—why they make heroes out of rock stars, movie stars, and other popular personalities who have made themselves available for adoration and emulation. In most cases, these are the adults who appear to identify with adolescents, who understand them, and who are, by adolescent standards, successful. They are not always young: many rock stars are in their forties and fifties! But in the absence of real-life adults who care about kids, rock idols fill the void.

A Stronger Bridge

While our earlier diagram showing the peer group to be the primary bridge from childhood to adulthood is an accurate description of the world we live in, we must add the fact that adults play an equally significant role.

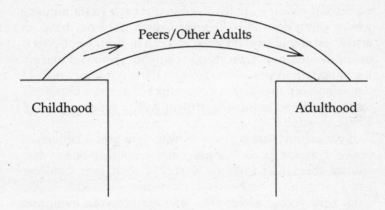

The bridge to adulthood is a relational bridge. <u>Young adolescents need people other than their parents who will help them mature and become independent.</u> They need many friends—peer friends, yes, but also *adult* friends. Most middle schoolers I know are thrilled when an adult other than their parents takes them seriously, listens to them, and affirms them in some way. Such an adult is given a great deal of power and authority over them because they are so special and rare.

When my daughter Amber was in the seventh grade, her favorite teacher always played classical music in the classroom while students were studying and doing class work. To my surprise, I noticed one evening that Amber was playing classical music in her bedroom while she was doing her homework. She did it because her favorite teacher—who liked her—did. To this day, Amber still enjoys listening (occasionally) to classical music while studying.

I am thankful that when I was a teenager there were some adults who cared about me and influenced me greatly. Even though they were few (I can count them on the fingers of one hand), they were extremely influential in my life. I am in youth ministry today because there was a youth worker thirty-five years ago who took a special interest in me.

Parents should do everything they can to make sure their adolescent children are involved in a church youth ministry where adults love kids. If your church does not have an active youth ministry, do what you can to start one. If that is out of the question, then change churches. Your children are too important to you and to God for them not to be involved in a fellowship that makes every effort to minister effectively to its youth and to surround them with a group of caring, Christian adults.

If your church has a youth ministry, support it enthusiastically. Pray for its adult leaders and encourage rather than criticize them. Get involved if you possibly can. Consider being an adult who befriends someone else's kid. If you work with young adolescents who are not your own, you will have a better understanding and appreciation for your own children—plus you'll have the chance to make a real difference in someone's life.

For that reason, I am also a believer in Christian schools. My wife and I have made financial sacrifices to keep our three children in Christian schools. We didn't make this decision because we wanted to protect our kids from "secular humanism" or non-Christian influences—I don't believe in "Christian ghettos." My wife and I simply wanted our children to spend the best part of their day around Christian adults who love Jesus and who love kids. I am thankful for the Christian teachers who have prayed for my children and spent many hours caring for them during the school day.

Not everyone has access to Christian schools or dynamic youth ministries. But all of us can take steps to surround our kids with adults who are good people and who are willing to share a little of themselves with our kids. That person can be a neighbor, a teacher, a coach, an aunt, or an uncle—anyone. Some churches have instituted an "adopt an adolescent" program which encourages every adult in the church to take one young person's name and pray for him or her on a regular basis. The adults remember their teen on his or her birthday and get to know that young person on a personal level. Such a program can have a powerful impact on kids who are looking for adults who will treat them with respect and take them seriously.

Choosing the Right Friends

I'll never forget Steve. He was a member of my junior-high youth group, and I liked him a lot. He was a good kid, with a lot of talent and potential. I tabbed him to play Joseph in our Christmas pageant one year, and he did a great job.

Steve stopped coming to church for no apparent reason, and I grew concerned. His parents weren't sure what was going on, but they were worried about some of Steve's friends. They didn't know who these kids were or where they lived, and Steve wasn't telling them much. When I finally caught up with him, Steve had changed. He was smoking and wearing the colors of one of the neighborhood gangs. I knew he was in trouble.

The next time I saw Steve, he was in juvenile hall. He and some of his friends had stolen a car and committed other crimes. This behavior ended up costing Steve several years as he was moved from one institution to another. I tried to keep in touch and let him know that I still believed in him.

Today, Steve is married, has two children, and is active in his church. He has started his own business and is doing well. Every time I see Steve, I'm grateful to God that Steve survived a difficult period in his life when he fell in with the wrong crowd. It happens to a lot of kids, and many of them never survive. They ruin their lives forever.

One of the fears all parents have is that their adolescent

children will fall in with the wrong crowd. Those fears are sometimes justified. It is very easy for kids to choose friends who do not hold Christian values and who may exert a negative influence on them. Kids who smoke, drink, use drugs, or engage in promiscuous or other kinds of negative behavior are often in the majority on a middle-school campus. It is natural to want to protect our children from these destructive behaviors and to encourage them to choose the right kinds of friends.

But in reality, we cannot choose our kids' friends. That's one of the decisions teenagers have to make on their own. As parents, we can and should offer guidance, but it is usually counter-productive to disallow, criticize, or put down the friends our middle-school children select. To do so is to attack their judgment and to show little or no faith in them. If you criticize your children's friends or try to prevent your kids from having the friends they want, you will have rebellion on your hands.

There are things we can do, however. When it becomes apparent that there may be dangers inherent in a particular relationship, we should certainly discuss our concerns with our child. But we should not assume the worst—as if anti-social or negative behavior is always contagious. Psychologist Eda LeShan offered this advice:

> There are times when it is a necessary part of growing up to live through a particular relationship. Much growth and learning about oneself can take place, even in some of the most ill-advised friendships. The only real protection against poor friendship choices is whatever help we can give our children in respecting themselves so much that they are unlikely to choose relationships that will hurt or demean them, and that we help them to understand enough about human motivation and behavior to judge others with insight.[10]

Adolescents (as well as adults) tend to choose friends from the same social tier as they see themselves. If young people perceive themselves as being at the bottom of the self-concept scale, then they will choose friends from that level. If they see themselves as high on the scale, they will choose friends who have a high self-concept and high standards of behavior. Dr. LeShan's advice is to treat your children as if they were higher up the scale. That improves considerably the chances that they will avoid choosing friends from the bottom. It's not a guarantee—but it's good advice.

Two developmental issues are at work here: (1) young adolescents need to make decisions on their own, and (2) they need to have friends. It makes good sense to allow middle schoolers to choose their own friends. When we do, it is more likely that our kids will include us in their circle of friends.

Remember that most of us made some poor choices in our friends when we were teenagers, and somehow we survived. Chances are pretty good that our kids will, too. Don't fear the friends that your children bring home. Get to know them and recognize that they serve a very important function. Make your home a place where your children's friends are welcome. Let them have parties and overnighters at your place, if it's possible. Observe, but don't intrude. And don't worry about the mess. Sure, there will be mud tracked all over the carpet and soft drinks spilled on the sofa. They will more than likely knock over and break your favorite lamp. And the noise will drive you crazy. But recognize that this is a small price to pay for providing a safe environment where your kids and their friends feel at home. It's better to know where they are.

The Value of One Good Friend

We would love it if all the friends our children chose were "good" friends—friends from good homes and good backgrounds who share the values and beliefs that we do. But that is unquestionably an unreasonable expectation. On the other hand, it isn't unreasonable to want our children to have at least one "good" friend. Sometimes that friend can make all the difference.

James Dobson once described an experiment that was done with a group of teenagers. The kids thought the experiment had to do with perception, but it actually had to do with peer pressure. A team of doctors asked a group of students to look at three cards, each with a line drawn on it, and to choose the longest line—line A, line B, or line C. The students were asked to raise their hands to vote.

What one student didn't know was that all the other students in the room had been secretly instructed to vote for the second-longest line. When the students held up their hands to vote, the uninformed student looked around the room in disbelief. Line B was obviously the longest, but everyone was voting for line A.

Seventy-five percent of the time, the uninformed students would vote with the rest of the group, even though they knew that the others were wrong. They didn't want to be different. They figured the crowd must know something that they didn't.

The study also found that if *one other student* voted for the correct line, then the chances were greatly increased that the uninformed student would hold his or her ground and not conform to the rest of the group.[11]

One of the benefits of a church youth group is that it helps kids find Christian friends and discover that they are not alone. They find other students who share their values and faith and will stand with them on their middle-school campus. A good youth group is a place where kids can make good friends—friends who can offer support to each other out "in the world" when they are faced with peer pressure and the temptation to conform. Sometimes all it takes is one good friend. Pray that your middle schooler has one.

Parents Can Be Friends, Too

We've discussed middle schoolers' needs for both peer friends and adult friends, but we haven't said much about the role of parents. You need to relate to your children in a

new way when they reach early adolescence. W.
are small, it's okay to relate to them from a positio
and authority. Children respond to that positive.
them a feeling of security. But adolescents are not i.
with power and authority. They respond to relation.   .iι
school, good teachers are teachers who are liked. Kids will
always perform well for teachers who have a good relationship with them. Similarly, if you want your kids to conform
to rules and standards that are important to you, do
whatever you can to build and protect your relationship with
them.

What is the best way to keep the relationship warm
between you and your young teens? Some people think it is
possible to buy a good relationship with things or money. I
know one teenage girl who attempted suicide after a bout
with depression. She was hospitalized for several weeks,
and during that time, her parents had her bedroom redeco-
rated. They thought that a new environment would make
their daughter feel less depressed. But their daughter
responded by saying, "I didn't need a new bedroom. I
needed them!"

As with most relationships, the best way to build a good
relationship with your middle schoolers is through dialogue.
Unfortunately, few parents take the time to enter into
meaningful conversation with their children on a regular
basis. Studies reveal that typical parents spend an average of
fifteen minutes a week talking with their kids.[12] Sociologist
H. Stephen Glenn observed:

> Interaction within nuclear families today has been reduced to
> only a few minutes per day. Of these few minutes, over half are
> used in one-way, negatively toned communications of parents
> issuing warnings or reproaching children for things done
> wrong.[13]

He's right. Evenings in most American homes have
changed in the last forty years from living rooms filled with
conversation to family rooms filled with TV sets and

Nintendo games. There is very little time for the positive interaction that results in healthy parent-child relationships.

I realized this was true in my own family a few years ago and took steps to do something about it. When my oldest son, Nate, was thirteen, I asked him if he would be interested in joining me for breakfast once a week. He agreed (since he loves to eat breakfast out). Every Wednesday morning, we got up early and went to breakfast. We had about an hour before school, and we used that time to talk. I tried not to scold Nate or lecture him or teach him anything. We simply talked like friends talk. For six years, until he graduated from high school, Wednesday morning was our morning. It made a significant difference in our relationship.

How do you have meaningful conversation with an adolescent? "Talk, don't communicate," suggested David Elkind.[14] That may sound like double-talk, but it's not. Talk with your kids without trying to *communicate* anything other than your willingness to talk. Most of the time, parents talk to their kids only when they have something significant to say—instructions, commands, warnings. But Elkind wisely advised to talk like you would to a friend. If you talk to your kids like you talk to other adults, they will be more likely to respond in an adult manner. If you talk down to your kids, they will usually respond in a childlike manner.

Another tip: Listen, don't lecture. Middle schoolers desperately want someone to listen to them. It makes them feel important. They want to be taken seriously, and the best way to take anyone seriously is to listen to them. That's why listening has rightly been called "the language of love."

Without question, the most common complaint I hear from teens about their parents is, "They *never* listen to me." You may wonder why your middle-school children will talk for hours to their friends, but will hardly say a word to you. One reason kids avoid talking to their parents is because they don't think anyone is listening.

I discovered years ago what a poor listener I was, so I had to learn some listening skills. One helpful device for me has been the acronym FAD. It stands for focusing, accepting, and drawing out. In order to be a good listener, you must first focus. Stop what you are doing and give your children your undivided attention. Most kids think their parents are too busy to listen to them. By focusing, you prove to your kids that they are more important than what you are doing. Second, show acceptance by smiling, leaning forward, and letting your children know that you are happy to be listening. Third, draw out your kids by asking questions and commenting on what you hear. Your desire for more information lets them know that you truly are interested in what they have to say.

Regardless of the method you use for listening, the important thing is to do it. Not only will you learn a lot and affirm your kids in the process, but you will also build a relationship with your middle-school children that will be the foundation for the relationship you have with them for the rest of their lives.

CHAPTER 4

A New Way of Thinking

"Dad, how fast are you driving?"

Dan was shocked by this unexpected query from his twelve-year-old son, Luke, as they were speeding down the freeway.

"Dad. How fast are you driving?" Luke asked again, only louder.

"Well, um, let's see . . ." (Dan glanced at the speedometer as if he didn't know that he was going well over the speed limit.) "Looks like, oh, about sixty-five, son. But we're not going too fast."

Luke folded his arms, turned slowly to his father, and said, "*Dad,* don't you realize that you are breaking the law? Don't you know what the speed limit is on this highway?"

Now Dan was getting angry. *How* dare *he correct my behavior,* he thought. *If anyone's behavior needs to be corrected, it's his! Since when does he think he can talk to his father like this?*

"Dad," Luke's insistent voice interrupted his father's reverie. "Don't you know that thousands of people are killed each year on the highway? Don't you care about my life or the lives of other people? Why are you going over the speed limit?"

"Luke, I told you we're not going too fast! Of course I care about you. Now be quiet. I don't need a back-seat driver!"

"But *Dad.*" Luke bit his tongue.

Dan was mystified. *What brought this on, anyway? Luke has never questioned my driving before. And in the past, if he asked why, I'd explain things and that was good enough. Why is he upset now?*

What Dan didn't realize was that Luke had just acquired some new thinking abilities. Things will never again be the same. Before, Dan could toss out pat answers and quick responses and have them accepted without question. But no longer. Now Luke can think, and he's going to need answers that make sense, and make sense to him.

As I wrote earlier, the key to understanding middle schoolers is taking seriously the reality of transition. We know that this transition occurs physically; the body changes so that it can function as an adult. Socially, we have seen how the middle schooler transitions from dependency to independence via the bridge of relationships. And while these definitive shifts are taking place in the physical and social areas, the young adolescent is also undergoing an exciting intellectual transition.

There are basic differences between the way a child thinks and an adult thinks. Perhaps this difference is what the apostle Paul was referring to when he wrote, "When I was a child . . . I thought like a child, I reasoned like a child. When I became a man, I put childish ways behind me" (1 Cor. 13:11).

During early adolescence most young people begin to develop adult understanding. A new world emerges—much more complicated than before, yet wonderfully exciting. Prior to age eleven or twelve, children's understanding of reality is largely tied to their experience. A qualitative change in understanding occurs often at about the onset of puberty. This change involves more than simply becoming more intelligent or learning more. Middle schoolers develop the ability to reason more logically, to conceptualize, to think abstractly, and to move from one abstract idea to another. They can speculate on the many possible effects of something they want to do. They can keep a lot of possibilities in their heads at one time, yet come up with an answer. These are all things middle schoolers were unable to do when they "thought like a child."

Meet Jean Piaget

A tremendous amount of research has been done in the last fifty years to discover how the brain develops. Probably the most widely accepted research in this field of cognitive development was done by the late Jean Piaget, a Swiss psychologist. Over several decades, he conducted numerous studies and made brilliant observations about the thought processes of children, especially about their ability to think logically. He noted that intelligence does not increase over time at a steady rate, but in spurts. The conventional IQ score often is not an accurate measure of intelligence because people shift from one stage of thinking to a higher stage at different ages.

Piaget's "stages of cognitive development" are levels of thought, each one more sophisticated than the one before. According to Piaget, people move from one stage to the next, never backward, as they mature. Piaget called the first stage the sensori-motor period. It is best characterized by infants, who do little or no organized thinking. They merely respond. Their perception of the world is obtained directly through their physical senses. By about age two, children have learned that actions have physical consequences and that they are not the same as their environment.

The second stage is called the period of pre-logical or pre-operational thought. It typically lasts from age two to five. The thinking of children during this stage contains a magical element—they are not able to distinguish well between events or objects they experience and those they imagine. Although things are beginning to make sense, these children still believe that everything in the world revolves around them. Language and other symbols develop at this stage.

The third stage is called the period of concrete operations. (An *operation* is defined as a logical thought process.) Here

85

children are not as ego-centered, but they still relate most things to themselves. Children between ages five and twelve are usually in this group. They learn to observe, count, organize, memorize, and reorganize concrete objects and information without losing the distinction between the real and the imaginary. They can figure things out for themselves and solve problems. The brain is much like a computer at this stage, processing information and making conclusions based on concrete data. Children are given many opportunities to use this ability in school. They learn facts and figures, the parts of speech, the names of all the presidents, and how to read and write and multiply and divide.

The fourth (and final) stage is called the period of formal operations. Most people enter this stage between age eleven and age fifteen (the middle-school years), if they are going to enter it at all. Piaget discovered that some people never do. But when kids reach stage four, they are able for the first time to deal with abstractions, to reason, to understand, and to construct complex systems of thought—to formulate philosophies, to struggle with contradictions, to think about the future, and to appreciate the beauty of a metaphor. This stage gives people the ability to perform operations on operations—to classify classifications, combine combinations, and relate relationships. One can "think about thought" and at the same time develop an awareness that knowledge is extremely limited.[1]

The shift from stage-three to stage-four thinking is much like seeing a color television set after having only known black and white all your life. A brand new dimension is added to a person's ability to think. David Elkind calls this newly-acquired ability "thinking in a new key," and he reminds us that it doesn't happen overnight.

It is important to remember that young people are as unfamiliar with their new thinking abilities as they are with their newly configured bodies. Moreover, thinking on a higher level takes time to get used to. Teenagers need to become accustomed to living in a new body. And just as they are often awkward in the use of their transformed bodies, they are sometimes equally awkward in the use of their new thinking powers. As adults, we have to be careful not to mistake their awkwardness in thinking, which may sometimes manifest itself in the form of insensitive remarks, for anything more sinister than inexperience.[2]

Graphically, Piaget's stages of cognitive development look like this:

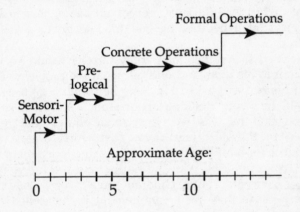

Charts and graphs don't always tell you how your own children are developing. Every individual is different and progresses at his or her own speed. Some kids will make the shift from concrete to formal operations at a very early age. But the majority don't manifest upper-level thinking until the eighth or ninth grade. Researchers have found that only about 30 percent of eighth graders in this country have completed the transition from concrete to formal operations; that is, they have shown the ability to handle intellectual tasks that require formal reasoning. But intellectual development is not always apparent by observation or testing. Sometimes you will notice a change in the way your children are thinking (like Luke, the back-seat driver), but not always.

Congratulations, You've Got Insomnia

One evening when my son Nathan was about thirteen years old, he went to bed at his usual time, around 9:30. But an hour or so later, he got up and complained that he couldn't go to sleep. We told him to go back to bed; he'd be asleep in no time. Another hour went by, and again we heard his footsteps down the hall. We warned him to go back to bed and get to sleep—or else! (After all, it was a school night.) A little later, he got up again, this time in tears, frustrated because he had tried to go to sleep but couldn't.

I decided that rather than apply force, I would go with Nathan into his room and find out what the problem was. I sat on his bed and asked him why he couldn't go to sleep. He said he kept "thinking about stuff." As we talked, I realized that he was worrying about things that might happen in the next few days. That worry was a new experience for him. Worry is, in fact, a stage-four experience. Worry concerns itself with the future, and the future is an abstract concept. Young children rarely worry about the future because they can't comprehend it. But when their intellectual capabilities advance to stage-four levels, kids discover that the future (and thus worry) have become all too real.

It's not necessary to completely understand Piaget's theories of cognitive development, but it helps to understand that middle-school kids are making an intellectual transition from child-like to adult-like thinking. Knowing this helped me understand why my son was experiencing insomnia, and I was able to be more empathetic. I didn't try to explain Piaget to him, but I did let him know that worry is a common experience. Most of the time, we worry more than we need to. I told him to try to think about something else for a while. He did, and he went to sleep.

As children acquire this new ability to think, they don't suddenly wake up brilliant. They simply begin to see things in a new way, and they acquire a new potential for reasoning. When your children reach this stage, the "inquisition" begins. You will have to defend all your values, rules, and behavior to them. They will recognize your inconsistencies, and when they do, look out. They'll usually let you know about them.

Try taking a couple of thirteen-year-olds to an amusement park and buying them a children's ticket (twelve-and-under) to save money. They will immediately let you know that they are no longer twelve and furthermore, it is wrong to cheat the amusement park by lying about your age. When they were younger, they would have taken the ticket and accepted it, no questions asked. But now? No way. They refuse to go along. When this happens, our tendency is to get defensive and try to use power and authority, but they interrupt and argue with us, and we end up getting angry: "Just do as I say!"

We need to remember that this behavior is not the same as defiance or rebellion. Actually, it gives us an opportunity to help our children develop their new thinking abilities. We can no longer give them easy answers and get away with it. When you say no to your middle-school children, you will need more than a simple no. You will need to explain the content of that no. They will want to know why or why not. And the answer you give will need to make sense to them.

This is sometimes difficult for us because we aren't used to relating to our children this way. Sometimes it takes us a while to make the transition in how we interact with them. One of the most common complaints middle schoolers make about their parents is that "they treat me like a child" or "they don't take me seriously." That's because they *were* children not so long ago, and it's tough not to keep seeing our kids as the little boys and girls who took orders and kept their mouths shut.

Once your children make the transition from concrete to formal thinking, encourage their questions and allow them to argue with you a little bit and exercise their new ability to process information. Middle schoolers need at least one person in their lives who will take time to help them develop this new potential. If kids are not encouraged and given opportunities to exercise their new intellectual abilities, they may never learn to ask the right questions or handle the academic expectations of high school.

One way to do this is to ask your middle schoolers lots of questions. When your children answer, don't settle for a one-word response or the shrug and grunt. Get them to elaborate on their responses by asking, What do you mean by that? or How do you know that is true? or That's an interesting answer; how did you come to that conclusion? Questions like these help develop upper-level thinking potential. If you can get your kids to defend or explain their thinking, you are doing them a service. If they don't respond to your questions right away, don't worry about it. They are not used to talking on that level. It will take time for them to become comfortable having adult-like conversations. But don't give up.

Another way to encourage our kids' new thinking ability is to allow them to make decisions about things. We dealt with this in chapter one, but it bears mentioning again. You can't continue to make all your kids' decisions. It's hard for us to break this habit because we made all the decisions when our children were younger. But with their new thinking ability and their great desire for autonomy, our kids can make more decisions for themselves. Give them that opportunity. You can help them process the information they need in order to make the decision, but give them the chance to make the decision itself on their own. When they make the decision, you can again ask questions like, How did you come to that conclusion? or Why did you decide to do that? This helps them to be accountable for their decisions. They will, by the way, ask you the same questions about your decisions.

Remember that as your children develop a new way of thinking, you will probably need to develop a new way of relating to them. If you continue to treat your middle schoolers as children, they will either respond like children (retarding their development) or rebel (destroying your relationship). You can affirm your children and build your relationship with them by treating them like adults, being honest with them, and allowing them into your world.

Bor-r-ring!

That's how Jennifer described her middle-school Sunday school class. "I'm not going anymore," she told her mother. "The teacher thinks we're all a bunch of little kids."

Actually, the Sunday school teacher is probably doing the best he can. If he has a classroom made up of sixth- through eighth-grade kids, he has a group of students who are all over the place developmentally. Some are slow developers, some are early bloomers, and most are somewhere in the middle.

If the Sunday school teacher relates to the class as if they were all on the lowest rung of the developmental ladder, he will lose many of them. Young adolescents who are learning to think in a new way will find old teaching methods extremely uninteresting and boring. They will become impatient and uncooperative. The same is true when a teacher tries to relate to students as if they were all upper-level thinkers. Kids who don't understand are going to rebel. It's no wonder that middle-school classrooms are notoriously rowdy. (Of course, adult classes would be rowdy, too, if the teacher were boring half the class to death.)

Kara, a youth worker at a church in our city, took a group of middle schoolers on a hike. The hike was designed for fun and as a way to teach kids a few things about nature and God.

At one point, the group came to a stream that was too wide to cross on foot. A rope had been tied to the branch of a tree, enabling the hikers to swing out over the stream to the other side. Kara used this opportunity to describe how the rope was like Jesus. The stream is like the sin in our life, Kara explained. Sin separates us from God, just like the stream separates us from where we want to be. But Jesus is like the rope—he makes it possible for us to get to the other side.

"Now swing across the stream on the rope, and remember, just as you trust the rope to carry you across the stream, so you must trust Christ as Savior."

It was a very effective lesson, but Kara noticed one of the girls off to the side, sobbing gently. Privately, Kara asked her what was wrong. The girl told her that she was afraid to swing across the stream on the rope, and therefore, she was afraid she could not be a Christian. "Do you have to swing on the rope to become a Christian?" she asked.

The girl was unable to make the leap from the concrete to the abstract. She hadn't yet made the transition from stage-three to stage-four thinking, and the lesson only confused and frustrated her. Kara assured the girl that she could be a Christian without swinging across the stream on a rope.

Teachers who work with this age group need to realize that some students will feel very uncomfortable dealing with abstract concepts and upper-level learning strategies. They will be frustrated and perform very poorly. They aren't ignorant or lazy; they simply haven't made the transition from concrete to formal thinking. A teacher who is presenting the story of Noah would be better off asking such students, How many days and nights was Noah in the ark? than, What lessons can we learn from the experience of Noah and his family? Stage-three learners would find the first question quite challenging and the second question frustrating. Stage-four learners, by contrast, would prefer the second question.

If your middle schoolers complain about school or church being boring, they are probably telling the truth. If the curriculum is too advanced for them, it is going to be boring. If it is too juvenile, it is also going to be boring. Finding the right mix for a group of middle schoolers is no easy task. The best thing we can do is give kids this age personal attention and make sure that they are "getting" what we are teaching.

We can't force kids to learn what they are incapable of learning, and we can't expect kids who are skilled at upper-level reasoning to stay interested in curriculum that doesn't challenge them.

I remember when my son Nate would come home from school with a list of vocabulary words to learn, many of which were very abstract. Nate had no idea what these words meant, and he understood even less the definitions that were provided. Helping him prepare for vocabulary quizzes, I would elaborate on the meanings of the words, so that he wouldn't have to memorize the definitions verbatim. It didn't work. I finally realized that the best thing for Nate was to memorize the definitions. He always hated those quizzes, and I don't blame him. The unfortunate thing is that since these words were covered in middle school, he never learned their meanings all the way through high school.

Adolescent Relapse

When you look at Piaget's stages of cognitive development, it may appear that children progress steadily forward, from one stage to the next. Such a view can be misleading. While intellectual development advances over time, the road is rather bumpy, with a number of turns and detours along the way. One of these detours, which commonly occurs during early adolescence, is called *adolescent relapse*.

It seems logical that with newly acquired mental capabilities, middle schoolers would be anxious to excel academically and to put their improved brainpower to work. The opposite is often true. For many (if not most) kids, the quality of schoolwork goes down during the middle-school years. Kids who performed very well in elementary school often do quite poorly when they reach adolescence, much to the dismay of parents and teachers alike.

There are several reasons why adolescent relapse is normal. As we just discussed, sometimes curriculum is

93

developmentally inappropriate, making school seem boring or unchallenging. Kids lose interest in learning.

But another important reason for adolescent relapse is the major distractions that kids view as more important than schoolwork. These distractions include sudden physical growth, rapid sexual development, the readjustment of relationships with adults and peers, and the quest for independence. A lot is going on in the life of middle schoolers. To expect smooth academic performance in the midst of such turmoil is to expect the impossible. It is not easy to make schoolwork fascinating enough to win out over these distractions. Not until their lives become more stable in the tenth, eleventh, or twelfth grade, do many young people develop a driving intellectual curiosity and pleasure from dealing with ideas.

Another reason for adolescent relapse has to do with motivation. Middle schoolers are not sufficiently motivated to perform at a high level academically. They are, in fact, "between motivations." When they were younger, your kids were motivated to do well because it pleased you. They would bring their papers home from school (hopefully with good grades on them), and you would proudly display them on the refrigerator door. This motivated your kids to continue to get good grades. When they get older, they will again be highly motivated by a desire to be better equipped for adulthood, to get a good job, or to expand their knowledge on a particular subject.

During early adolescence, however, kids are between motivations. They are neither motivated to please their parents, nor motivated to prepare themselves for adulthood. Instead, they want to explore the world, try things out, make friends, have fun, and experience all they can.

In recent years, some middle schools have begun experimental programs allowing students to participate in local community service projects rather than going to class. Students are delivering hot lunches to shut-ins; working in soup kitchens, day-care centers, and hospitals; and learning a good deal more than they would in a classroom situation. They are developing self-esteem and learning responsibility—plus they are learning what life is like for people from other generations and in other situations. To quote one teacher who is involved in the program, "This is how middle-school students learn. They don't learn by having a teacher tell them to be caring, but by seeing how it feels to be caring."

Such programs have much to commend them. Middle schoolers learn a great deal from personal experience. If your kids are bored with school, it is probably not experiential enough. Take your children out of school, if necessary, so that they can be involved in service or experience new things. I travel quite a bit, and I frequently allow my kids to accompany me on trips so that they can meet new people and visit new places. They learn many things from experiences like these. A wise man once told me, "Don't let school get in the way of your children's education." This is especially true for middle schoolers.

Pseudo-Stupidity

Psychologist David Elkind has written much to help us better understand why young adolescents act and feel the way they do. Drawing from the work of Piaget, Elkind has identified and named several characteristics of adolescent behavior stemming from the shift from concrete to formal operations.[3]

The first of these Elkind calls "pseudo-stupidity," the tendency of young adolescents to interpret and respond to situations in a much more complex manner than is warranted. While everyone does this to some extent, it is most common in middle schoolers. The obvious seems to elude them. When trying to solve a simple problem, they tend to look for the answer in the least obvious places. In school, they may approach subjects at a much too complex level and fail, not because the tasks are too difficult but because they are too simple.

Pseudo-stupidity arises because when young adolescents make the shift to formal operational thinking, they aren't able to control their new abilities. The capacity to weigh many different alternatives is not yet coupled with the ability to assign priorities and to decide which choice is most appropriate. Consequently, young adolescents often appear to be stupid when, in reality, they are too bright.

Kids at this age may see complex, devious motives in the simplest or most accidental behavior of their friends, teachers, parents, brothers, and sisters. A simple discussion with a middle schooler can become extremely complicated and sidetracked by the young adolescent's overeager intellectualization of the issue at hand. This may result in miscommunication, misunderstanding, frustration, and, more often than not, hurt feelings.

Thirteen-year-old Marcus, for example, can't find his shoes. His favorite pair of Nikes are missing, and until they turn up, he is going to make everyone's life miserable. Marcus is a bright kid, but his behavior seems, well, stupid. Rather than looking for his shoes in the obvious places— under his bed (where they are) or outside on the front lawn where he tends to leave his stuff—he will rehearse in his mind all kinds of scenarios which have his evil sister hiding his shoes from him or someone stealing his shoes as part of some sinister plot to ruin his life. He will sweat bullets trying to come up with a complex explanation for the loss of his shoes to avoid punishment from his parents. The simple thing would be for him to look under the bed. But that's too easy.

Delia Ephron offers a good example of pseudo-stupidity in her book *Teenage Romance*. A teenage girl is complaining to her mother about a midnight curfew.

> "Oh, Mom, come on. Nobody gets home that early, nobody! Do you want me to be the only kid in the entire group that has to leave early? The only one who can't stay out? Do you? Do you

want me to ruin everybody else's time because I have to leave because my mom doesn't trust me while everyone else's mom does? Is that what you want? Is it? Great, just great. You're really getting impossible, you know that? You've changed, Mom, you have. You never listen, you never try to understand. You just give orders—do this, do that. . . . You never let me do anything I want. Never. If you had your way, I'd be in jail. You know, you're ruining my life. Probably no one will ever invite me anywhere again as long as I live. I'll probably never have another date. I'll spend the rest of my life in my room!"[4]

Everybody's Looking at Me

Have you ever listened to two middle schoolers talk on the telephone?

"Hi Tiffany, this is Janie! Hey, what are you wearing to school tomorrow? . . . I've been thinking about wearing my red leggings with my mom's white sweater and some big red dangly earrings that I got at the mall last week. What do you think? . . .

"Do you think Billy likes me? Sometimes I don't think he even notices me . . . What a jerk I made of myself today at school, I just don't believe what I did. I know everybody must think I'm a total geek!"

These conversations rarely have much to do with world events, the future, philosophical questions, long-range planning. No, middle schoolers usually talk about themselves—how they look, how they feel, what others think of them, what they are going to do to impress this guy or that girl. They seem terribly egocentric.

But that's another characteristic of middle schoolers that comes because of the advent of formal operations. Elkind has called this kind of egocentrism "the imaginary audience." Young adolescents play to an audience that they imagine is watching them all the time. This characteristic accounts for our kids' extreme self-consciousness.

Where does this egocentrism come from? Essentially, when young teens acquire the ability to think abstractly, it opens up the possibility to "think about thought." As they think about thoughts, they also think about other people's thoughts. This new ability, however, is coupled with the inability to distinguish between what is of interest to others and what is of interest to them. Since middle schoolers are primarily interested in themselves, they assume that everyone else must also be interested in them. They begin to think that everyone around them is as concerned with their appearance and behavior as they are. They feel like they are constantly on stage. They surround themselves with an imaginary audience.

This helps explain why young teenagers spend so much time in the bathroom primping and combing their hair. When they stand in front of the mirror, they imagine how everyone else will see them and what they will think. Everyone does this to some extent (don't you?), but with young adolescents, it can seem obsessive.

This characteristic also explains why middle schoolers feel such a need to show off or to engage in disruptive or destructive behavior. In many respects, such behavior is a performance. Kids are playing to the crowd. When middle schoolers vandalize, for example, they are probably thinking more about the reaction of their imaginary audience than about what they are destroying.

Fortunately, this kind of behavior tends to decline with age as young people come to realize that other people have their own problems and concerns. There comes a time when you have to accept the fact that other people don't (and can't) care about you as much as *you* care about you. But until middle schoolers' perspective on this becomes more realistic, their imaginary audience is very real indeed.

We can help our middle schoolers learn to differentiate between their own concerns and the concerns of others by taking a middle-ground position. If our children say that nobody likes them, we shouldn't tell them that they are wrong and that people really like them. It would be better to say, "Well, I like you. And frankly, I can't understand why others wouldn't like you, too. What do others say or do that makes you feel that way?" This type of approach helps kids test their feelings against reality and see the world as it is.

It Can't Happen to Me

Adolescents are well-known as risk-takers. Professionals talk a great deal about at-risk youth, and the consensus is that all youth are at risk. This view stems not only from the fact that there are many dangerous activities and enticements luring kids into risky behavior, but also because teenagers are at a stage of life when they seem unable to make rational decisions about their behavior.

Elkind attributes this to a unique form of egocentrism which he calls "the personal fable." It says, "I am a special case; I am unique." While our children are special and unique, the personal fable distorts reality to the point that kids see themselves as immune to the things that happen to other people. *Others will grow old and die, but not me*, kids think. *Others will get pregnant and have to drop out of school, but not me; others will get AIDS, but not me.*

Again, the advent of formal operational thinking contributes to this form of egocentrism. Middle schoolers are able to conceive the future (an abstract concept, because it doesn't yet exist), but many tend either to deny it or to idealize it. Teenagers who hold an extremely pessimistic view of the future may live for the present moment because they feel powerless to change the future. It is so grim that they simply ignore it. Others, however, idealize the future and envision their future as unrealistically bright. They can't envision themselves poor, sick, in jail, or dead. *Bad things happen to other people, but not to me.*

This is why it is often futile to talk to kids about the consequences of their behavior. They simply don't believe such bad things will happen to them. They think they will always be the exception. When kids get into accidents, get pregnant, or get involved with drugs, they haven't chosen to accept the consequences of their actions—they never thought those consequences would happen to them.

The personal fable is at work when you hear middle schoolers say, "You don't understand me. You just don't know what it feels like!" They believe their feelings and needs are so unique that they are beyond the realm of anyone else's understanding, including their parents'. Sometimes this can make communication very difficult, particularly when you are trying to let your children know that you really do understand.

Again, the best way to help middle schoolers outgrow this unrealistic view of themselves is to encourage them and to help them check their version of reality against that of others. Ask questions. Help your children think through the decisions they make and the behaviors they choose to engage in. Rather than argue with them or deny them their perceptions of themselves, help them see that other people are special, too. This approach helps kids distinguish between the ways in which they are like others and the ways in which they are different. The more they are encouraged to think about themselves and their future in a realistic manner, the more responsible they will become.

A more stop-gap approach is to help kids recognize and appreciate the short-term consequences of their behavior. For example, a recent stop-smoking campaign for middle schoolers tried to convince kids that smoking spoils your looks. Posters featured ugly people (rather than glamorous people) smoking cigarettes. This campaign got much better results than campaigns that taught kids the long-term health benefits of a smoke-free lifestyle. If kids understand that a behavior has short-term consequences that are better avoided, they are less likely to engage in that behavior. Parents are well-advised to set up a system of logical consequences that encourages the behavior they expect from their teenage children and puts teeth into their rules.

None of these characteristics (pseudo-stupidity, the imaginary audience, the personal fable) are by any means new.

But by naming them and understanding why they occur, we learn to be more empathetic and less judgmental. It is common to attribute the worst possible motives to behavior we don't understand. If we recognize that such behavior is due in large part to the intellectual immaturity of our middle-school kids and not because they are dumb, selfish, or crazy, then we can respond in a rational, helpful manner that leads to maturity and positive growth.

CHAPTER 5

An Emotional Roller Coaster

Cheerleader tryouts for Roosevelt Middle School are tomorrow morning. Angela has practiced her routines, and she just knows she's going to be selected this year.

Angela has borrowed a cheerleader outfit from a friend. It fits perfectly, but she needs the right shoes. Her parents have agreed to let Angela buy them if she pays half, so Angela has saved her money and has a pair all picked out at the shoe store downtown.

Her father, Tom, agreed to pick her up after school and take her to the shoe store, so when the last period bell rings, Angela dashes out to the flagpole, anxiously waiting for her father.

Tom is delayed at work for forty-five minutes. Forty-five minutes may not seem like a long time to most people, but to a middle-school girl waiting to buy cheerleader shoes, it seems like an eternity.

When Tom finally arrives at school, he apologizes for being late, but Angela explodes. "I've been waiting and waiting!" she screams. "You *said* we would go right after school! The shoes are probably *gone* by now and it's all your fault!" With that, she furiously throws her books into the backseat, slams the car door, and bursts into a fountain of tears.

Tom isn't sure how to respond to this outburst. He's torn between anger and sympathy, with a touch of guilt for being late. If he had been on time, this probably wouldn't have happened. Still, he decides, his daughter has no right to talk to him like this.

"Angela, I want you to stop this right now. I told you I was sorry for being late, and there's still plenty of time to buy your shoes. But I think perhaps the best thing for us to do right now is go home. We're not going shopping for anything while you are acting like this."

Tom starts the car and tries to think of a good way to handle the situation once they get home. Some punishment is necessary for Angela's behavior, and there's still the problem of the shoes—if and when to buy them. Mostly, Tom is feeling discouraged and frustrated.

"Dad?" says a sweet, small voice.

He turns and looks into the beaming, smiling, tear-stained face of his daughter. "Dad, are you mad at me?"

Welcome to the emotional roller coaster that is early adolescence. Angela's behavior is typical of middle schoolers who are, by adult standards, extremely emotional people. Because many of them have acquired the ability to think in a new way, they also have acquired the ability to feel in a new way. They have emotions that are not only new to them, but also extremely intense and completely unpredictable. Middle schoolers can go from an incurable case of the giggles to anger or withdrawal in an instant—for no apparent reason.

While such behavior is typical, we must understand that, emotionally, there is no such thing as a typical middle schooler. Within a group of fifteen to twenty middle schoolers, there may be a few kids who are boisterous and loud, others who are quiet and moody, and still others who are timid and withdrawn. Myriad peaks and valleys clutter the emotional landscape of early adolescence. These kids run the gamut of emotions and moods and usually don't begin to learn how to control their feelings until later in adolescence.

Like other areas of life we have described in this book, emotional development in middle schoolers reflects the transition they are undergoing from childhood to adulthood. More accurately, emotional changes are the *result* of changes

104

taking place in other areas. Children's approach to their early adolescent years depends on the intellectual, physical, and social systems that have supported them for eleven or twelve years. Suddenly, much that they have come to depend on starts to change. Their bodies grow and develop; friends and outside interests compete with the security previously found in the family; their views of the world begin to change as their minds develop; and their emotions begin to flip-flop like Mexican jumping beans. A once stable world suddenly feels like it's made out of Jell-O.

Emotions are a reflection both of what is going on in our kids' lives and of their maturity. Since each person responds to situations and circumstances in his or her own way, it is practically impossible to predict how a group of people (especially middle schoolers) will integrate their emotions with their behavior. One middle schooler may experience a great deal of stress in a given situation, while a, other kid may have no difficulty with it at all. Some middle schoolers seem to be sitting on an emotional powder keg, while others show an unusual amount of emotional stability and are able to take almost everything in stride.

Unfortunately, the word *emotion* suggests agitation and excitement. We tend to think of emotions as a strange force mysteriously arising from nowhere to seize and control individuals. This extreme view exaggerates the dramatic and disturbing aspects of emotions and fails to acknowledge that much of adolescent emotional life is calm and constructive. A person can be quite emotional without flying into a rage, crying hysterically, or being silly. Emotions are always present, no matter what behavior a person displays.

Even though emotional development is a secondary characteristic of early adolescence, the emotional instability of this age group concerns and frustrates parents because middle schoolers' emotions are likely to be translated into some kind of action. They don't hide their emotions well, even when they try. If middle schoolers feel lousy, they will usually let you know in some creative way. They may try to make everyone around them feel lousy. This can make life interesting for families with middle schoolers.

Emotions to the Max

One way to describe the emotions of young adolescents is to say that they are intense. These kids take emotions to the max. There's no middle ground, no halfway mark. Everything is either one extreme or the other—it is the best thing that ever happened or the worst. Something is either superior beyond compare or totally worthless. Because of this, middle schoolers give events and problems an importance out of proportion to their actual significance. A broken romance, failure to make the team, or poor grades may result in depression so severe that it leads to suicide—the number-two killer of young adolescents in the United States. Problems that adults view as ordinary may cause adolescents intense emotional distress leading to eating disorders, truancy, delinquency, drug and alcohol abuse, or complete withdrawal.

Emotions are so intense during early adolescence primarily because they are new. As middle schoolers gain an adult way of thinking, they also gain adult emotions, which are unlike those they had as children. It takes a while to get used to these new feelings and be able to control them. So when middle schoolers feel good about something, they are often ecstatic. When they are in love, they feel a greater love than anyone could comprehend.

As an eighth grader, I plastered my bedroom walls from floor to ceiling with my girlfriend's name and wrote her name over every square inch of my schoolbooks, homework papers, desktops, tennis shoes, ball gloves, and anything else with space enough to write. When we broke up, I wept bitterly. It was a tragedy of monumental proportions. Of course, it didn't take too long for someone to take my old girlfriend's place.

So it goes with the emotions of young adolescents. Unlike

adults and older teens, they fail to cope with their feelings realistically or consistently; instead, they surrender to them.

The emotions of middle schoolers can be explosive as well as deep. At times, their discontent with themselves and others will express itself in anger, and that anger is often expressed physically rather than verbally. If something happens that these kids don't like—let's say a person bumps into them or calls them a derogatory name—they may lash out and throw a punch. Middle schools deal with considerable fighting between students, and the girls are often just as violent as the boys.

Anger against adults often expresses itself in outbursts ending in tears. Middle schoolers will stomp their feet, slam doors, and throw things. Some kids will lock themselves in their bedrooms or run away from home (although they usually come back in a short while).

I ran away from home when I was in seventh grade. I was furious with my parents and wanted to teach them a lesson. I was gone for a couple of hours, figuring that by then my parents would be frantic and would have called the police. I heard a siren in the distance and knew it was the police looking for me. *I'll bet my parents are really sorry that they treated me so badly*, I thought. I finally went home (because I was getting hungry), only to discover that nobody had noticed my absence.

The anger of a middle schooler can be highly explosive and difficult to deal with. It's tough to be rational and reasonable with an angry, tearful girl or boy. The best way to deal with an angry middle schooler is to be understanding and wait it out. Their emotions are short-lived.

Remember that middle schoolers are learning to deal with their emotions. Their feelings are not that different from yours. In the example that began this chapter, Angela's father was also experiencing a wide range of emotions. Unlike his daughter, Tom could draw from experience. He thought about his options before he acted on his emotions, and he tried to separate how he was feeling from what he did.

We can help our middle schoolers process their feelings in a similar fashion. Remember that emotions are valid, no matter what they are. Kids should not be punished or scolded for having emotions. Feeling angry or impatient or energetic or depressed is not inherently wrong. The problem arises when the anger leads to violence or the energy leads to being disruptive or disrespectful. Kids need to know that even if they can't control their feelings, they *can* control what they do with their feelings. Never punish feelings, only behavior. This is the basis for teaching children self-control.

Of course, one of the best ways to teach emotional control is to model it in front of our kids. There will undoubtedly be times when we get very angry with our kids, and it is then that we need to make sure that we are responding in a rational, adult manner. If you blow it, admit your failings and apologize. Not only will this keep your relationship warm, but it also teaches kids honesty and humility.

One day a few years ago, I got very angry at my son, Nathan, for something he had done. (I don't remember what it was.) I yelled at him, and he yelled back at me (which made me even angrier), and I lashed into him with a series of expletives and threats that I don't use on adults, let alone my children. His short-lived anger turned to despair, and he started to cry. I suddenly realized how out of line I was. It had been a very stressful week at work, and I was taking my frustrations out on my son. I was wrong to hurt him the way I did.

As he stood with tears streaming down his face, I put my arms around him and asked him to forgive me. We cried together for a little while. Afterwards, I sat down with him and tried to explain a little of what I was feeling. Having shared a painful experience, we were able to talk and listen to each other with a deeper level of understanding. That experience was one of the worst and best that ever happened to us as father and son.

Jekyll and Hyde Personality Development

Mr. Detheridge, the seventh-grade math teacher, hated to see it happen. After all, Chad was one of his favorite students.

As recently as a month ago, Chad was performing at an above-average level. He seemed enthusiastic about math and was always willing to solve problems on the board. He was getting good grades and was a delight to have in class.

But for the past several weeks, Mr. Detheridge has watched Chad change. When he's called on to solve problems, he refuses. He isn't turning in his homework, and he's talking out of turn in class and causing serious problems with a few other disruptive students. Mr. Detheridge has had to send Chad to the principal's office twice.

When Chad's parents discovered what was going on, they naturally were concerned. They met with Mr. Detheridge to discuss the situation and assured him that there were no major problems in Chad's life that they could identify. Mr. Detheridge suggested a few ways to encourage Chad to do better in school, but his principle advice was this: "Be patient with him. Chances are pretty good that he'll decide he liked himself better when he was a good student. He'll probably come around soon enough."

What Chad's parents found out from that meeting was that sometimes Mr. Detheridge's entire seventh-grade class behaves in this way. During the course of the year, good students become bad students, and quiet students become talkative students. Lazy students become hard workers, and helpful students become problem students. "Being a seventh-grade math teacher is a challenge" was how Mr. Detheridge put it.

It is not a good idea to make too many generalizations about middle-school kids, especially about their emotional and psychological development. Emotional unpredictability sets these kids apart from the rest of the human race. Adults and little children can normally be put into categories without too much difficulty: She's such a pleasant little girl;

Mr. Jones is a happy-go-lucky sort of guy. Middle schoolers, on the other hand, may be pleasant today and quite nasty tomorrow.

When I was leading youth groups, I commonly had students who were cooperative and enthusiastic one week and inexplicably belligerent and disruptive the next. I finally decided that this was normal behavior. With middle schoolers, the abnormal is the normal. I've seen aggressive hostility and childlike submissiveness in the same meeting from the same student. The young person who is talkative and open one moment might suddenly clam up altogether. Some people may wonder if these kids are victims of some psychological disorder. They aren't. They are simply being themselves.

Adolescent psychologists offer a reasonable explanation for this bizarre, unpredictable behavior that may offer some consolation. It certainly helps us understand what is going on, even if it doesn't alter the situation much. The explanation goes this way: In the process of adolescent development, middle schoolers essentially "try on" a variety of personalities for size to see which one or ones fit them best. They develop their personalities through a process of trial and error. They will express a variety of emotions, feelings, attitudes, and temperaments to discover the range of reactions they get from others, especially their peers. If the reaction is favorable, the behavior may be repeated; if it is not, the behavior may be discontinued. They also try on various emotions just to see if the feelings fit. When a middle schooler gets angry and throws his lunch across the cafeteria, he will decide whether or not that person was really "him." If he is comfortable with his anger, he may harbor it for a while. If he doesn't particularly like how he felt, then he may discard that feeling and go on to another.

This explanation may be an oversimplification, but it gives us a framework for understanding what is going on with our kids. It is consistent with what we know about the primary tasks of early adolescence. As young people make the transition from childhood to adulthood, they are trying to come up with their own identity. The personality, like the body and the mind, is being shaped during this time and is probably in its most unstable period.

This is why it is not at all unusual for youngsters to act like extroverts one day and introverts the next. They are trying to see what they will be most comfortable with as adults. Middle schoolers may try all sorts of personalities—the class clown, the hood, the brain, the teacher's pet, the quiet type, the spoiled brat, the flirt—before their distinctive personality traits begin to emerge. These kids haven't committed themselves to a particular personality pattern, but most of them will be making that commitment in only a few years. If a middle schooler gets positive feedback from others by acting a certain way and feels comfortable doing so, this behavior will no doubt continue.

Negative feedback usually acts as a deterrent. Keep in mind, however, that negative feedback from adults may very well be interpreted as positive feedback by middle schoolers. This possibility complicates things when you are trying to encourage or discourage behavior.

In case all of this sounds like some insidious adolescent game, keep in mind that our kids are not aware of their subconscious, trial-and-error, personality-shaping process. Kids don't wake up in the morning and say to themselves, "Yesterday I tried my warm and friendly personality; today I'll see how my mean and nasty one goes over." It happens naturally and involuntarily. The process is quite dramatic in some kids, and hardly noticeable in others. It's important to remember that every young person is different.

The Need for Stability

How do we respond to the emotional ups and downs of early adolescence? Perhaps the best way is to provide a measure of stability for our kids during these years. In other words, it serves the best interests of both you and your

111

middle schoolers to be consistent. When your children were younger, you could get away with saying one thing and doing another, with changing your mind about what they could or couldn't do or what the consequences would be for a particular behavior. Now you need to be more consistent.

One way you can do this is to sit down with your spouse and decide what you expect of your middle schoolers and what your rules and standards are going to be. You need to decide how you are going to handle situations before they happen. It is important for the home front to be united on issues such as dating, curfew, friends, grades, social activities, allowance, dress and appearance, chores, television rules, drugs and alcohol, and church participation. I'm not suggesting that you create a huge list of rules and regulations for every possible situation; only that you come to some agreement on what is important and what is not. Choose your battles wisely, or you will be battling all the time.

Some things are not worth fighting over. They are a waste of energy, not to mention being counter-productive. Psychologist James Dobson has suggested what he calls his "loosen and tighten" principle. As children grow older, you loosen your grip on things that have no moral significance, and you tighten your grip on things that do.[1] It may no longer be prudent to waste your energy on battles over messy bedrooms or hairstyles. Save your energy for important issues such as drug and alcohol use or dating rules. A good rule of thumb is to say yes to your children whenever you can in order to give support to the occasional no.

It's important for parents to agree on what issues are worth fighting about with their kids and to apply discipline consistently. If you need to, take a weekend with your spouse and discuss these issues.

Another way to provide some consistency is to follow through on your promises and consequences. If you promise your middle schooler that you will take him fishing on Saturday, take him fishing on Saturday. If you warn her that she will be grounded for two weeks if she breaks curfew, enforce that consequence. Unlike more mature adults, middle schoolers do not always allow a grace period for inconsistent behavior. Once a promise is broken or a consequence is ignored, they simply decide that your promises and warnings are meaningless.

A consistently-applied program of logical consequences is the best way to discipline adolescents. They are too big to spank, and scolding goes in one ear and out the other.[2] Decide what your rules are, and then create logical consequences that will be enforced if the rules are broken. If you have a rule that your children's homework must be finished before they watch television, decide what will happen if that rule is broken. You might ask your kids to think of a consequence that sounds reasonable. Then you simply apply that consequence whenever a rule is broken. Follow through on your word, rationally and respectfully. But remember that whenever possible, the consequence should be agreed upon before, not after, the infraction occurs.

Another way to provide stability for your middle-school children is to avoid allowing your own instability to spill over into their lives. Psychologists agree that external changes should be minimized when children are experiencing many internal changes, such as they are during their middle-school years. These years are especially bad for major external changes such as parents divorcing or a move to another city. Parents of young adolescents often face significant changes in jobs, life-styles, and priorities. Some of these are unavoidable. But keep in mind that it is best for middle schoolers when the world around them is as stable as possible while the world inside them is changing rapidly.

One more thought on this subject. The most stabilizing influence you can provide for your children is unconditional love. There will be times when your children will quite literally hate you. They can become uncontrollably angry and say things that they (and you) will probably regret. As parents, we are tempted to respond in kind or take their anger and hatred much too personally. Our feelings get hurt,

113

and we become alarmed, concerned, and angry. But we must never shut the door on our kids. We must never cut them off in a way that gives them the message that we don't love them anymore.

I have heard many teenagers brag about fighting with their parents, but I have never heard a teenager brag that his parents no longer loved him. Such knowledge is more than most kids can handle without suffering serious psychological damage. Love will always draw them back.

Richard Foster, in his book *Prayer: Finding the Heart's True Home*, tells a charming story about a man who was walking through a shopping mall with his two-year-old son. The child was in a particularly cantankerous mood, fussing and fuming. The frustrated father tried everything to quiet his son, but nothing seemed to help. The child simply would not obey.

Then under some special inspiration, the father scooped up his son and, holding him close to his chest, began singing an impromptu love song. None of the words rhymed. He sang off key. And yet, as best he could, this father began sharing his heart. "I love you," he sang. "I'm so glad you're my boy. You make me happy. I like the way you laugh."

As the father continued singing off-key and in words that didn't rhyme, the boy relaxed and became still, listening to this strange and wonderful song. Finally they finished shopping and went to the car. As the father opened the door and prepared to buckle his son in the car seat, the child lifted his head and said simply, "Sing it to me again, Daddy! Sing it to me again!"[3]

We never outgrow our need for unconditional love. Maybe that's why the most beloved of all of Jesus' parables is the story of a forgiving father and his rebellious, misbehaving teenage son in Luke 15. Jesus told this story to describe how God deals with his wayward children, but it also stands as a compelling model for parents of teenagers. Never lock your kids out. Leave the door wide open, learn the art of forgiveness, and communicate unconditional love.

Am I Okay?

Mark Twain once said, "I can live two months on one good compliment." Most of us could use more than that, but the sentiment is true: We need affirmation and encouragement in order to live successful and happy lives.

If that's true for you and me, it is even more true for middle schoolers. The most pressing psychological task of early adolescence is to build self-esteem. As we discussed in chapter three, the big question on the minds of middle schoolers is, "Do you like me?" These kids want to know if they are accepted by others, if they are okay.

Young children have few self-esteem problems—or at least, they shouldn't have. Good parents generally shower their children with praise and make them feel like they are the only children in the world. This is as it should be. An environment of extravagant affirmation and attention provides children with security and safety.

But as kids approach adolescence, they realize that the security of the home and the security of the world are two different things. As they begin to seek independence and venture forth from the protection of their home, they want to know if they are going to be liked out in the real world as much as they are liked at home. They need to discover if they have what it takes to survive on their own.

Family therapist and former youth worker Bill Wennerholm has identified a number of steps that young people must take to build their self-esteem and become healthy adults. These steps are part of a gradual process that usually takes several years.

1. The establishment of emotional and psychological independence from parents.
2. The achievement of a separate personal identity.
3. The ability to motivate oneself and set one's own goals and direction.
4. The development of one's own values and beliefs.
5. The ability to be in intimate reciprocal relationships.

6. The establishment of an appropriate sexual identity, which includes accepting and appreciating one's own unique body.

7. The ability to function in a work capacity.[4]

Each of these steps takes time and requires the cooperation and feedback of others, including parents. Notice that none of these steps is directly associated with self-esteem. That's because true self-esteem is not contrived or pumped up. It is a by-product of healthy development. Self-esteem comes, in the words of the commercial, "the old-fashioned way." It has to be earned.

H. Stephen Glenn and Jane Nelsen, in their book *Raising Self-Reliant Children in a Self-Indulgent World*, offer a similar list which they call "The Significant Seven"—three perceptions and four skills which all children must acquire in order to have healthy self-esteem and to function as capable, responsible adults.

1. A strong perception of personal capability. ("I am capable. I can do things by myself.")

2. A strong perception of personal significance. ("I contribute in meaningful ways and I am genuinely needed.")

3. A strong perception of personal power. ("I can influence or control what happens to me. I am not just a victim of circumstances.")

4. Strong intrapersonal skills. The ability to understand personal emotions and use that understanding to develop self-discipline and self-control and to learn from experience.

5. Strong interpersonal skills. The ability to work with others and develop friendships through communication, cooperation, negotiation, sharing, empathizing, and listening.

6. Strong systemic skills. The ability to respond to the limits and consequences of everyday life with responsibility, adaptability, flexibility, and integrity.

7. Strong judgment skills. The ability to use wisdom and evaluate situations according to appropriate values.[5]

In the past, these perceptions and skills were acquired naturally. Children were surrounded by adults and extended family rather than by peers. They were given meaningful roles in the family and community rather than just hanging out or flipping burgers. Leisure time was spent interacting with adults rather than watching television and playing Nintendo games.

We have to find other ways to help our kids feel capable and self-reliant, able to control their lives and influence their world. We do this not by nagging and imploring, but by treating our kids with unusual dignity and respect, giving them more—not less—of our time and attention, and offering them all the help and encouragement we can. Children are not going to learn to become adults from other children. They need parents who believe in them and are willing to do what it takes to help them succeed on their own.

The best place to start that process is by keeping your relationship with your children warm. Let them know that you not only love them, but you like them as well. When your children enter the room, what do they see? A frown or a smile? It is important to let kids know that you are happy to see them and enjoy their company. Further, they need to know that you believe in them, trust them, and take them seriously. One of the most effective ways to do this is by listening. When you give middle schoolers your undivided attention, you let them know that what they have to say is important and that you value them.

Another excellent way to help young adolescents build their self-esteem is to encourage them with words. Sadly, many middle schoolers long for a "Home on the Range" where "seldom is heard a discouraging word." Instead, they hear, "How many times do I have to tell you!" "Grow up!" "Why can't you be like your sister?" "You *never* do what I tell you!" "Where did you get a stupid idea like that?" Scripture encourages parents not to discourage children but to build them up (Colossians 3:21). Say something positive to your middle schoolers whenever you can—and avoid putting them down or attacking them needlessly.

Try some of the following phrases on your children. If

necessary, practice them in front of the mirror just to get used to them and see how they sound. All of them can be used to encourage your children and to build their self-confidence and self-esteem.

I love you.
How thoughtful.
I know you can do it.
That's a good point.
You're terrific.
That's great!
It sounds like you've given that a lot of thought.
Now that's an interesting way of looking at things.
You are really improving. I'm proud of you!
I know you'll make the right decision. I trust you.
That was a thoughtful thing to do.
That's okay. Nobody's perfect.
Since you're not happy with the situation, what do you
think you can do to change it?
Let's sit down and talk about it.
Now, that's really creative!
You really are growing up!
Way to go!
You made the right decision.
I've noticed that you've really been trying harder.
Thanks for your help.
You handled the situation well.
Good thinking!
I really appreciate you!
That's a normal feeling that you have.
I'm going to trust you a lot more.
Will you pray for me?
I'm sorry. Will you forgive me?
What's your opinion?
It's easy to make a mistake. What did you
learn from it?
I understand.
I love you.

Some of these phrases are designed simply to give kids positive feedback from their experiences. It is important to let kids know when they do something right. Not only does it make them feel good, but it also encourages them to continue with that kind of behavior. Be liberal with praise. Catch your kids in the act of doing something good. Most young adolescents are so used to being scolded, nagged, criticized, and ridiculed that they think they have a sign on their back reading, "Kick me, I'm in middle school."

Compliment your middle-school kids whenever you have the opportunity. And when you compliment them, emphasize positive character traits rather than possessions or appearance: "I really appreciated the way you helped out last night," rather than "That's a great-looking shirt!"

Don't hesitate to compliment your kids in front of other people. Even though they may act uneasy and embarrassed, deep inside they are taking their bows and basking in the glory of it all. Kids really do want their parents to be proud of them.

CHAPTER 6

Finding a Personal Faith

No one is quite sure how it started, but everyone thinks they know who started it. While the congregation was pausing for silent prayer and meditation, a muffled, choking noise like someone trying to contain a cough carried across the sanctuary. Suppressed giggles sounded from the front of the church. Within a few seconds, a group of middle schoolers seated in the first three pews erupted in laughter.

According to one twelve-year-old eyewitness, it started when "somebody cut the cheese," although he declined to identify the guilty party. Some believe it was the elder who tried to introduce a resolution at the next church board meeting to ban middle schoolers from all worship services where adults are present. "These children are not capable of understanding the things of God," he said. "They are not only irreverent, but they are spiritually bankrupt."

Unfortunately, many people share the view that spirituality and middle schoolers are mutually exclusive. It's hard for them to imagine young adolescents sitting reverently in church, listening attentively to the pastor's sermon, singing enthusiastically, and discussing theological issues with each other. Perhaps they have difficulty imagining it because, to my knowledge, it never happens. When it comes to spirituality, middle schoolers don't behave like adults. But that doesn't mean they aren't interested in spiritual things. Middle schoolers are in the process of finding a faith that makes sense to them—a personal faith. It's important for us to understand that process and to encourage it in a positive direction.

The Man on the Flying Trapeze

As we discuss the spiritual development of middle schoolers, we must understand that it is in transition. The spiritual dimension of life cannot be set apart from the rest of life as if it were an entity unto itself. Faith touches all areas of life—the physical, social, intellectual, and emotional. We have already discussed the major changes that are taking place in those areas during the middle-school years. Each of those changes affects the spiritual lives of middle schoolers.

Because their bodies are changing and growing, middle schoolers become increasingly aware of their mortality and the scriptural imperative to "offer your bodies as living sacrifices, holy and pleasing to God" (Romans 12:1). It will take years for them to become secure enough in their physical development to be able to understand the full meaning of that phrase.

The social dimension of life is also involved in spiritual development. When we talk about spirituality, we are describing a relationship with God. The goal of spirituality, after all, is to allow God to have the primary relationship in one's life.

As with other relationships (a marriage, for example), spirituality also includes both intellectual and emotional components. On an intellectual basis, it is necessary to understand what the relationship is about, who the relationship is with, why the relationship is important, and what commitment is being made. Emotions accompany and validate the relationship. These feelings can be described with words such as love, passion, affection, romance, infatuation, adoration, devotion, joy, and ecstasy. Most couples need to feel romantic love at least once in a while to have a successful marriage, but they also require a healthy dose of intellectual commitment to their spouse and to the concept of marriage itself. Likewise, one's spiritual life is both an emotional experience (feelings) and an act of the will (beliefs).

During my years as a youth worker, many concerned parents have come to me with questions like, "What's happening to my daughter? She used to love church and Sunday school. Now she doesn't want to go. She complains that its boring and stupid. She doesn't seem to be interested in spiritual things anymore. What have we done wrong? How can we prevent her from losing her faith altogether?"

Usually my first response is to encourage patience. I like to compare a middle schooler's faith to a man on a flying trapeze. A trapeze artist will swing on one trapeze for a time, then let go of it in order to "fly through the air with the greatest of ease" and reach a second trapeze some distance away. The audience always gasps and holds their breath while the man makes his transition from one trapeze to the other—it seems so risky and dangerous. If you took a photo of the man in transition, it would appear that nothing was supporting him. He is hanging in mid-air. But more often than not, the trapeze artist grabs onto another trapeze which looks a lot like the one he left behind, and all is well. In the same way, young teens often let go of their childhood faith in order to grab on to another one—the faith that will carry them into adulthood.

It is wise for parents to trust that this process is good for their children. Middle schoolers, in their quest for autonomy, need to let go of the faith of their childhood (the faith of their parents, in most cases) and grab on to a faith that is their own. They will do this in time, and more often than not, the faith they adopt as their own will look a lot like the faith they left behind.

David Elkind offered a comforting observation: "In general, most young people return to the faith of their parents once they become young adults and particularly when they become parents themselves."[1] There is an old saying that goes, "Don't worry if your children reject your value system and advice now; someday they will offer it to their own children." There are never any guarantees, of course, but generally speaking, that saying holds a lot of truth.

You Expect Me to Believe That?

Erica was sitting in her usual place Sunday morning as the Sunday school teacher began leading the class in the song, "God Is So Good." Erica had sung that chorus hundreds of times, but this time she was having a hard time singing along. *God is so good. What does that mean, anyway?* she wondered. *Since when has God been good to me? I've been praying for Mom to get well, but she's only getting worse. And ever since Daddy lost his job, we haven't had any money for anything. I was hoping for some new shoes for school, but now Daddy says we can't afford it. What money we have goes for medical bills. Where is God anyway? Doesn't he care about my family?*

Erica is not unlike many young adolescents who have questions and doubts about their faith. Young children have a simple, almost mythical faith—one that provides clear-cut answers to life's most difficult questions. It provides them with invincible heroes of the faith to admire and emulate. They believe because their parents and their teachers believe. But with the advent of adulthood and the ability to think on an adult level (formal operations), kids sense that the faith of their childhood won't do. They don't want to be embarrassed by what they believe. Instead, they want a more mature faith, one that is personal and makes the transition from childhood to adulthood along with them.

Unless we are willing to help children discover this faith, we are in danger of losing them during their early adolescent years. Many middle schoolers reject their faith and lose interest in church simply because they are still being asked to believe in a God whom they have literally outgrown. We need to help our children see God in a new light and see how their faith in Christ relates to the world that is opening up before them.

Young adolescents will have many questions when they reach the middle-school years. They don't always have the courage or motivation to verbalize them, but they have questions nonetheless.

When Jesus was a boy, his parents took him to Jerusalem for the celebration of Passover (Luke 2:41-52). When they left to go home, they discovered that Jesus was missing. (Apparently Jesus was seeking a little autonomy of his own.) When Mary and Joseph finally found him, he was in the temple, asking questions of the teachers who were there. Like most Jewish children, Jesus had been instructed in the Scriptures, but when he got older, he had questions. It is no surprise that these questions came gushing out when Jesus was twelve years old.

Our children are no different, although they usually don't make a beeline for the church and start quizzing the pastor. As young adolescents move from stage-three to stage-four thinking, they begin to question much of what they have been taught in the past. Their new capacity for thinking things through and coming to their own conclusions makes it necessary for them to reaffirm the learning they acquired from their parents, teachers, and peers. They want assurance that it is really true. They will often spot inconsistencies and contradictions that they hadn't seen before or that hadn't bothered them before.

Adolescent psychologist Jerome Kagan explained one common way in which teens struggle with apparent inconsistencies.

> The fourteen-year-old broods about the inconsistency among the following three propositions: (1) God loves man. (2) The world contains many unhappy people. (3) If God loved man, he would not make so many people unhappy.
>
> The adolescent is troubled by the incompatibility that is immediately sensed when he examines these statements together. He notes the contradictions and has at least four choices. He can deny the second premise that man is ever unhappy; this is unlikely for the factual basis is too overwhelming. He can deny that God loves man; this is avoided for love of man is one of the

qualities of God. He can assume that the unhappiness serves an ulterior purpose God has for man; this possibility is sometimes chosen. Finally, he can deny the hypothesis of God.[2]

Despite the oversimplification, this example is typical of how young adolescents privately work out their own values and beliefs. They have been told that premarital sex is wrong, yet they find pleasure through sexual experiences. Is pleasure therefore wrong? They have been told that God answers prayers, yet they prayed and nothing happened. Why? Many young adolescents are dismayed to find themselves facing an endless stream of problems that force them to adjust their beliefs. Left alone, adolescents grow more and more skeptical, assuming that religious truth is nothing more than wishful thinking. Sometimes this leaves them temporarily without a commitment to any belief.

Of course, there are always a certain number of kids who will have no doubts whatsoever (no serious ones, anyway) and who will remain absolutely faithful throughout their early adolescent years. We can be thankful for them. These young people will simply build upon the foundation of their childhood faith. Still, they will need to modify their old beliefs and increase their understanding of them. Quite a few other kids will have nagging doubts about their faith but be afraid to express them. This group is probably larger than the faithful. Young adolescents generally lack the self-confidence necessary to express these feelings openly, so they tend to keep them locked inside.

If we understand that questioning and doubting is normal for this age group, we won't panic when our children experience or express pangs of disbelief, disinterest, or skepticism. There is no need to attempt to eliminate their doubt. We can help our middle schoolers by letting them know that their doubts and questions are permitted, that we are not to be afraid of them in the least. Certainly no question is too difficult for God. Questioning and doubting are necessary parts of one's spiritual development. "Doubts are the ants in the pants of faith; they keep it alive and moving," wrote Frederick Buechner.[3] Kids need to be assured that while they may doubt God and find him confusing and distant at times, God never doubts them.

Middle-School Martyrs

Early in my youth ministry, I worked for Youth For Christ, conducting Christian Bible Clubs on junior-high campuses. Since we were not allowed to meet on the campus itself, I borrowed a church bus and tried to have our meeting in the bus, parked in the school parking lot. I would pull the bus in the parking lot after school, and when the bell rang for the last class, I would wait on the bus for the kids to show up. I was always disappointed that only a handful would come— and those who did come were quite nervous about it. They would sneak around the cars in the parking lot, quickly jump on the bus, and then slump down in the seats so nobody would see them. After a few weeks of this, I realized that the bus was a big mistake. Asking students to climb on that bus in full view of their friends was like asking them to be fed to the lions in the Roman Coliseum.

Some people are quick to criticize Christian kids for their unwillingness to "take a stand for Jesus," but I think to criticize young adolescents for their lack of boldness is unnecessary and unfair. Middle-school kids aren't ready to sacrifice their fragile self-image and acceptance by their peers for their faith—at least not when their faith requires them to look foolish. Stepping onto a church bus parked smack dab in the middle of the school parking lot is hardly a require-ment for following Jesus. In retrospect, I don't blame those kids for not coming to my meetings. When I was that age, I probably would have stayed away, too.

Their reluctance to be publicly associated with Christian activities doesn't mean middle schoolers are less-than-Chris-tian or hypocritical. They simply have a need—at least for the time being—to keep their faith under wraps. Middle schoolers are in the middle of a very important task in their lives: making friends. Once they become more comfortable with who they are and confident that they are likable, they will be more willing to risk their relationships for the cause of Christ. But for now, don't be surprised when your middle schoolers balk at opportunities to "be a witness" and to take a public stand for their faith. To make such a public commitment at this age is a monumental act of courage.

That middle schoolers avoid taking public stands for their faith doesn't mean they lack faith. They are developing a much more personal faith than they had as children. When they were younger, their faith was more of an institutional faith—a faith that was defined by going to church, being in meetings with other people, learning stories. But now, faith becomes a private, personal matter. It evolves from an activity to a relationship with God. "Teenagers, who value their privacy, now that they have discovered that they can live in secret in their heads, and who are afraid that their secrets might be found out, discover that a personal God is a most trustworthy confidant. He won't squeal," wrote David Elkind.[4]

Middle schoolers are not always demonstrative about their faith in God, but their faith is alive, growing, and real, nonetheless. Recent research has found that 95 percent of adolescents aged eleven to fourteen believe in God, and that 75 percent pray every day.[5]

Who's Gonna Be There?

Alicia's parents were surprised when she said that she didn't want to go to the youth group retreat. Alicia always enjoyed going to Pine Cove. And this year's youth retreat featured one of Alicia's favorite musical groups.

"None of my friends are going," said Alicia.

"But it's going to be a wonderful retreat," urged Alicia's mother. "The youth pastor has put a lot of work into it this year."

"I don't care," said Alicia flatly. "I'm not going unless

Jennifer and Angela go. They're not going, so I'm not going."

Maybe you have had a similar conversation with your middle schoolers. Most parents have. Alicia, like other young people her age, wants to be with her friends, and that will be the deciding factor in what she chooses to do. Some people say that this is deplorable—that this is simply yielding to peer pressure—but that's not quite accurate. While peer pressure has something to do with decisions like these, the fact of the matter is that Alicia wants to be with her friends.

Relationships are very important to middle schoolers, and the presence or absence of friends can make any activity, no matter how good it is, wonderful or terrible. If you go to a rock concert and see ten thousand kids, ninety-five percent of them will be there not because of the rock group, but because of their friends. The same is true for church. Kids will be motivated to attend church or youth group functions because of the relationships that are offered.

In a survey I conducted several years ago of more than 750 middle schoolers, I asked, "Do you like school?" The overwhelming response was yes. When I asked why they liked school, the answer was almost unanimous: "Because that's where my friends are." Those who didn't like school gave a parallel response: "Because I don't have any friends" or "Because that's where my enemies are." Their answers had little to do with the wonderful school facilities or the excellent curriculum or the outstanding teachers. Friends were always the key issue.

James Fowler is a pioneer in the field of faith development. He has, like Jean Piaget, identified a series of stages that people pass through on the way to developing a mature, adult faith. We won't examine each of Fowler's stages here, but it is instructive to note how Fowler's third stage, which he calls "Synthetic/Conventional," is described.

This stage usually begins at eleven or twelve years as the person's experience is extended beyond the family and primary social group. It can last long into adulthood, and for some it becomes a permanent home. A stage three faith interprets, relates to, and makes meaning out of life according to the directions and criteria of what "they say," in other words, according to popular convention. It is a "conventional" or "conformist" stage in that it is anxious to respond faithfully to the expectations and judgments of significant others. As yet the person is without a sufficient grasp of his or her own identity to make autonomous judgments from an independent perspective.[6]

Fowler's research and work in the field of faith development only confirm what we observe. Friends are very important to young adolescents and determine much of what they do, say, and think. This is normal and to be expected.

That is why it is important for us to do whatever we can to provide friends and mentors for our kids who will be able to motivate them to right behavior and right beliefs. Let me emphasize again the importance of finding a church home for your family that has a youth ministry which provides friends and mentors for your kids. A good youth group is a place where your kids can find good friends—both peer friends and adult friends. There is no better way to help kids come to faith than through their relationships.

Consistently Inconsistent

Tom, the youth pastor at First Church, felt good about the series on mission and service that he did with his middle-school youth group. He challenged his students to prioritize their lives in such a way that they would always take into consideration the needs of others—the poor and the suffering.

The youth group responded wonderfully. During discussions and the commitment service, the students declared their "radical commitment" to not be selfish, to serve the less-fortunate, to contribute generously of their time and resources, and whenever they had the opportunity, to share God's love with others.

A few weeks later, Tom's middle-school youth group

conducted a fund-raiser which netted almost five hundred dollars. Tom thought it would be a good idea to let the students decide how the money would be spent. He gave them several options.

Among the options was the youth group's trip to Magic Mountain, an amusement park. The money would help buy tickets and provide transportation. Another option was to help support a mission project in Mexico. The money would help build a home for a family who were left homeless after the winter floods. Tom knew that this decision would be difficult for his middle schoolers, especially after their series on mission and service.

But it wasn't a difficult decision at all. The youth group voted unanimously to use the money for the Magic Mountain trip.

What happened to the commitment that this group made to serve the needy and to give to the less fortunate? Were they pretending to be committed to these values? Are they now being hypocritical? Not at all. They meant what they said when they declared their commitment to the poor and needy. They really did benefit from learning about missions and service. The problem is that these kids are not very good at connecting what they learn and believe (or say they learn and believe) with what they do. In other words, they don't practice what they preach.

David Elkind uses the term "apparent hypocrisy" to describe this characteristic of early adolescence. In his words, "They can be very idealistic, and 'talk a good game,' as the expression goes, but they usually fail to carry out the actions that would seem to follow logically from their professed ideals."[7] Unfortunately, this makes them look like hypocrites—people who say one thing and do another.

But they are not being hypocritical in the same way that we would think an adult hypocritical. Ordinarily, when an adult shows hypocritical behavior, we assume that he or she understands that it's inappropriate to say one thing and then do something that is obviously contradictory. But middle schoolers have not yet developed the ability to relate theory to practice or faith to works. This is why a thirteen-year-old can express strong views about what is fair or honest and then, without a moment's hesitation, act in a very unfair and dishonest manner.

I have listened to my thirteen-year-old son climb all over his sister for taking things out of his bedroom and using them without his permission, and then—on the same day— he'll take my tools off my workbench and use them without my permission (and I have told him numerous times not to do that.) It would be unfair for me to conclude that my son is a hypocrite. It will simply take some time for him to learn that there needs to be a vital and consistent relationship between what he believes and what he does.

If we were honest, we would empathize with our kids more on this point. We all have trouble connecting what we say or believe with what we do. Jesus recognized this as a recurring problem for his disciples and continually urged his followers to be "doers" of the Word, and not just "hearers." As adults, we have a tough time putting into practice what we believe, even though we've had years of experience. Our middle-school children are just beginning to walk down that path. They will become more consistent with time, but for now, they may look like hypocrites.

This also explains why young adolescents sometimes live two lives: acting like a Christian at church and acting quite the opposite at home or in school. Those two lives may be completely different from each other and very inconsistent, but the middle schooler living them will not perceive that there is a problem—or at least not a serious one.

Obviously, the Christian life requires a connection between faith and everyday life. It is not enough to believe. True though this is, we must be patient with young adolescents and recognize that they are doing well to express their values and beliefs verbally (if they do). For them, simply believing or conceiving a particular belief is a big step in the right direction. In time, they will discover the need to back up those beliefs with their actions.

We can help our kids learn this by being gentle with them. We can point out inconsistencies to them or help them to see those inconsistencies for themselves, but we need to let them know that we understand how difficult it is to do the right things sometimes. Encourage them to try again—to think before they act, asking themselves if what they are doing is the right thing to do. If we are overly judgmental, we run the risk that our kids will become frustrated and abandon their beliefs rather than work on their behavior.

We can also give our children opportunities to be "doers of the word." They will understand the connection between faith and works much better if they experience it themselves. This kind of experiential learning is sometimes called *praxis*, a term taken from the Greek word for "action." It is one of the best ways to teach middle schoolers. If you want your children to understand that we serve Christ by serving others, do more than talk about the concept. Give your kids an opportunity to serve. Perhaps your family could help distribute food at a rescue mission or visit people in a convalescent home or do yard work for shut-ins. Help your kids see first hand how your family's beliefs translate into action.

Here I Am, World

I have always enjoyed the inherent idealism of young adolescents. In spite of their awkwardness and their propensity to bungle things, they really believe that they are capable of doing anything they set their minds to. Generally, they haven't yet had their dreams and ideals ripped out of their hearts by discouraging people or discouraging experiences. As they begin their transition into adulthood, they are hopeful and optimistic about the future. They are extremely idealistic. They have a strong desire to be committed to something and to make their lives count. It is not uncommon for middle schoolers to list as career choices occupations such as doctor, nurse, missionary, teacher, or a worker with the handicapped. These professions reflect their desire to make a difference in the world.

Researchers have confirmed that middle schoolers are motivated by a desire "to do something important with my life."[8] In the words of Joan Lipsitz of the Center for Early Adolescence, these kids are "omnipotent in imagination, but impotent in action." They have a keen desire to do something important with their lives, but they have few opportunities to do so. As a result, they become discouraged, and they begin to believe that they are incompetent and useless.

As we discussed earlier, today's young teenagers have no "place" in society, as they did in the past when they took on apprenticeships or had family responsibilities. And the word on the street is that middle-school kids are too immature and too irresponsible to do meaningful work or to make a meaningful contribution to society. This perception explains why there is virtually no job market for middle schoolers. On the other hand, these kids are the nation's baby-sitters. Almost every eleven- to fourteen-year-old earns extra money by baby-sitting.

The irony of this situation is that often the people who consider these kids to be so immature and irresponsible are the same people who entrust their most prized possessions—their babies—into the care and safekeeping of sixth-, seventh-, and eighth-graders. Either these young people are in fact responsible, or adults are acting irresponsibly by leaving them alone with their babies.

I choose the first option. Middle schoolers are capable of accepting some responsibility, and they should be given every opportunity to do something important with their lives. The same kids who won't pick up their dirty clothes off the bedroom floor will often jump at the chance to do something for someone who needs help.

Millions of young teens across America have nothing to do after school except hang out, watch television, or get into trouble. Some of these are latchkey kids, who come home to empty houses because they live with one parent, both of their parents are working, or their parents don't care about them. We are well-advised to do what we can to help our middle schoolers find meaningful after-school activities, such as mission and service projects, apprenticeships, volunteer work, sports, and the arts.

Hey, I'm Alive Right Now

Twelve-year-old Rachel was puzzled. She and the rest of her youth group had just completed a mission project in the city, serving sandwiches and soup to the homeless. They were proud of what they had accomplished. As a result of their witness for Christ, several people had indicated their desire to become Christians.

On the Sunday morning following their service project, the pastor recognized the students from the pulpit, praising them for their good work. Then he made the statement that puzzled Rachel: "Young people," the pastor declared, "never forget that you are the church of tomorrow!"

Church of tomorrow? Rachel wondered. *Do we have to wait until tomorrow to be accepted as part of this church? Doesn't he know we're alive right now?*

Rachel's point is well-taken. Middle schoolers want to feel needed now, not later. It is essential that we give them opportunities to serve and to use their God-given gifts. Their idealism, strong though it may be, will diminish if it's not expressed. We need to find as many ways as possible to channel the energies and enthusiasm of our kids into positive activities that allow them to give of themselves and to see the results of their efforts. They need to feel the significance and affirmation that comes from doing things that are worthwhile and that benefit others.

Some kids feel that they were hopelessly short-changed when God was distributing the talents, gifts, and abilities necessary for becoming a "somebody" in his scheme of things. A certain degree of discouragement might set in when they compare themselves with biblical or historical heroes of the faith, popular Christian celebrities of today, or adult Christians they know, such as the pastor or the youth minister. Despite a genuine desire to accomplish much and to serve in some way, they often have the overriding fear that they are miserably unqualified and ill-equipped.

We can help middle schoolers know that God can and will use them just the way they are. I like to tell kids a story about a little girl who wanted to become a great pianist, but all she could play on the piano was the simple tune "Chopsticks." No matter how hard she tried, that was the best she could do. Her parents decided after some time to arrange for a great maestro to teach her to play properly. Of course, the little girl was delighted.

When the little girl and her parents arrived at the maestro's mansion for the first lesson, she climbed up onto the piano bench in front of the maestro's concert grand piano and immediately began playing "Chopsticks." Her embarrassed parents implored her to stop, but the maestro encouraged her to continue. He then took a seat on the bench next to the little girl and began to play along with her, adding chords, runs, and arpeggios. The little girl continued to play "Chopsticks." The parents couldn't believe their ears. What they heard was a beautiful piano duet played by their daughter and the maestro, and amazingly enough, its central theme was "Chopsticks."

Young adolescents need to be assured that although they may only have "Chopsticks" to offer God right now, he sits on the piano bench beside them. Just as Jesus took a boy's lunch beside the Sea of Galilee and used it to feed a multitude, he can take their "little" and turn it into "much." That's the way God works most of the time. Keep on playing!

More Is Caught than Taught

An important factor in the spiritual development of middle schoolers is whether they know people whose

Christian faith they can model. Most of what a young person learns about the Gospel and about life in general is passed on by example. Therefore, it is important to surround middle schoolers with people they can look up to and who will inspire them to follow Jesus Christ, the ultimate model for all of us.

The need for models is one of the reasons young adolescents are such hero-worshipers. They are easily led (or misled) by anyone who is able to capture their admiration and allegiance. In many cases, this amounts to near worship of teen idols, singers, and actors who are marketed directly to this age group in the media and elsewhere. Educators Howard and Stoumbis explained models this way:

> This is the time for admiration and imitation of the hero figure, which makes it important that the proper figures for emulation are presented to the adolescent. While their parents and teachers are no longer likely to be the persons to be imitated and admired, partly because of their fallibility, familiarity, and authority symbols, the young adolescent will still seek an older model to emulate—preferably one who is competent and successful by his adolescent standards.[9]

It makes good sense to point our young people toward models who are willing to identify themselves with Jesus Christ. They don't have to be famous or talented, although I am glad there are Christian recording artists and Christian sports figures who have become successful and accepted by the teenage crowd. We need more of these people.

But even more important than celebrity Christians, we need adult role models who care about our kids. As we discussed in chapter three, young adolescents need and want adult friends who are willing to lead them across the bridge from childhood to adulthood. I encourage and pray for the adults in my church because I recognize that they are role models for my children.

Recently while I was out of town on a trip, a good friend of mine invited my son to go with him on a ski trip for the weekend. I was delighted, not only because it provided a weekend activity for my son, but because it also provided an opportunity for my son to spend some time with a good man who cared about him and who was modeling the Christian faith in front of him.

Of course, we parents are in the best position to be positive models for our kids. Our choice is in what type of model we are. Like it or not, we are either positive or negative models. Our kids are watching us and learning from us about the Christian faith and life in general.

What do they see? What do they hear? I don't want to lay a guilt trip on anyone, but the simple fact is—our kids notice who we are and what we do. That doesn't mean we have to be perfect, of course. I like to tell people that my wife considers me to be a "model husband." That may sound pretty good, but look up the word *model* in the dictionary. It's defined as "a small imitation of the real thing." In a sense, that's all a model is. It isn't an exact duplicate of a particular ideal, but an often-imperfect representation that tries to be faithful to the original and points to it. That's what the Christian life is like, and our kids need to see that.

Remember: The best research we have continues to confirm that parents are the most important influence in the lives of their adolescent children. Your kids are watching you, and they are learning from you. As parents, we communicate to them a great deal more than we realize. Even when kids are "rebelling" or deliberately rejecting what we say and do, they are paying us more attention and learning a lot more from us than we think. That's why it is so important that we not lose our nerve and that we communicate the messages that we want them to receive.

We need to let our children know what is important to us, what motivates us, and why we believe the things we do. That doesn't mean we should preach or lecture to our kids. Preaching is not effective with teens. Rather than preaching at them, we share beliefs within a relationship.

As a parent, I want my kids to know what makes me tick, but I am no longer in a position to force my beliefs on them. I want to keep the communication lines open so that we can discuss important issues, and I also want them to see that my values and beliefs make a difference in my life. That's where the modeling comes in.

Beyond that, we need to pray continually for our kids. A friend of mine once told me, "When my children were young, I talked to them a lot about God. But after they became adolescents, I started talking to God a lot about my kids." That's good advice.

Ultimately, we need to trust God with our kids. God loves them more than we do, and he understands them better than we do. He created them and loves them with a perfect love that far surpasses our love for them. He understands parenting, too. After all, God had an adolescent Son, who grew up in the city of Nazareth and as a twelve-year-old increased "in wisdom and stature, and in favor with God and men" (Luke 2:52). Even though Jesus' adolescence is sometimes called "the silent years" because the Bible doesn't give us much information about that time, we can be assured that our Father in heaven has first-hand knowledge of all that we are experiencing as parents. Pray every day for your children.

Smile, You Have a Middle Schooler

We've come a long way since the beginning of this book. We started out by describing the myth of the teenage werewolf that often causes us to expect the worst and then get it. But the reverse is also true. If you look forward to your children's middle-school years and enter them with understanding, anticipation, and joy, then you can maintain a warm relationship with your kids and encourage them toward a positive adolescent experience.

That's why I believe one of the most important things we can do for our children at this age is to smile at them. When your middle schoolers enter the room, what message do they receive? Are you happy to see them? Or do you act cold, angry, or indifferent? We communicate volumes with our attitude and our disposition. A great man once said, "If you truly believe the Gospel of Jesus Christ—that it really is good news rather than bad news—then please, notify your face."

It is difficult to smile when your children have disobeyed or have become very demanding or have disappointed you in some way. When your children are middle schoolers, you can (if you choose) be angry or upset about something twenty-four hours a day. But you have another option. You can communicate joy in the midst of the grief.

Things will never be perfect with a middle schooler in the home, so if you are perfectionists, you may need to adjust your expectations. The perfectionist credo is "I would rather be right than happy." You may almost always be right, but if you can't live with a few wrongs now and then, you will not only be unhappy parents, but you will also make life miserable for everyone around you. Learn to live happily in the midst of a less-than-perfect world. Our kids need that from us. A smile on a parent's face gives them hope.

Adolescence is not terminal. It is a new birth, the beginning of an exciting transition into adulthood that you and your kids can experience together. You really can enjoy your middle schooler.

NOTES

Chapter 1: The Wonder Years

1. Marie Wynn, *Children Without Childhood* (New York: Penguin, 1983), 36.
2. Peter Benson, Dorothy Williams, and Arthur Johnson, *The Quicksilver Years: The Hopes and Fears of Early Adolescence* (San Francisco: Harper & Row, 1987), 10.
3. *The Random House College Dictionary*, rev. ed. (New York: Random House, 1982), 1120.
4. John A. Rice, *I Came Out of the Eighteenth Century* (New York: Harper & Row, 1942), 132.
5. Erik Erikson, *Identity, Youth, and Crisis* (New York: W. W. Norton, 1968), 91.
6. Ibid., 23.
7. H. Stephen Glenn and Jane Nelsen, *Raising Self-Reliant Children in a Self-Indulgent World* (Rocklin, Calif.: Prima, 1989), 161.
8. "Madison Avenue's Call of the Child," *U.S. News and World Report* (March 20, 1989).
9. *Minnesota Student Survey Report 1989* (Minneapolis: Learner Support Systems) quoted in *Youthworker Update* (March 1990): 3.
10. Search Institute, "Young Adolescents and Their Parents," *Project Report* (Minneapolis: Search Institute, 1984), 12.
11. Erikson, *Identity, Youth, and Crisis*, 54.
12. Ben Patterson, *Waiting* (Downers Grove, Ill.: InterVarsity Press, 1989), 162.
13. Victor Stursburger, quoted in *Youthworker Update* (September 1990): 1.

Chapter 2: The Perils of Puberty

1. Gilman D. Grave, *The Control of the Onset of Puberty* (New York: John Wiley & Sons, 1974), xxiii.
2. Ibid., 409.
3. J. M. Tanner, "Sequence, Tempo, and Individual Variation," in *Twelve to Sixteen: Early Adolescence,* ed. Robert Coles, et al. (New York: W. W. Norton, 1972), 22.
4. David Bromberg, Stephen Commins, and Stanford B. Friedman, "Protecting Physical and Mental Health," in *Toward Adolescence: The Middle School Years,* ed. Maurice Johnson (Chicago: Univ. of Chicago Press, 1980), 140.
5. David Elkind, *All Grown Up and No Place to Go* (Reading, Mass.: Addison-Wesley, 1984), 93.
6. Quoted in Elkind, 49.
7. Search Institute, "Young Adolescents and Their Parents," 101. See also J. Norman and M. Harris, *The Private Life of the American Teenager* (New York: Rawson-Wade, 1981).
8. Robert Coles and Geoffrey Stokes, *Sex and the American Teenager* (New York: Harper & Row, 1985), 2.
9. Judy Blume, *Letters to Judy* (New York: G. Putnam's Sons, 1986), 166.
10. Elkind, *All Grown Up,* 5.
11. Search Institute, "Young Adolescents and Their Parents," 88.
12. "How Should We Teach Our Children About Sex?" *Time* (May 24, 1993): 63.
13. Quoted in Coles and Stokes, *Sex and the American Teenager,* 2.
14. Coles and Stokes, *Sex and the American Teenager,* 38.
15. Search Institute, "Young Adolescents and Their Parents," 14.
16. Coles and Stokes, *Sex and the American Teenager,* 38.
17. Blume, *Letters to Judy,* 155.
18. "So Who's Counting?" *Youthworker Update* (May 1987): 4.

19. Joan Lipsitz, *Growing Up Forgotten* (Lexington, Mass.: Lexington Books, 1977), 17.

Chapter 3: Making Friends
1. Lipsitz, *Growing Up Forgotten*, 122.
2. Delia Ephron, *Teenage Romance* (New York: Viking, 1981), 32.
3. Joan Lipsitz, "The Age Group," in *Toward Adolescence: The Middle School Years*, ed. Mauritz Johnson (Chicago: The National Society for the Study of Education), 14.
4. Alvin W. Howard and George C. Stoumbis, *The Junior High and Middle School: Issues and Practices* (Scranton, Penn.: Intext Educational Publishers, 1970), 34.
5. Search Institute, "Young Adolescents and Their Parents," 97.
6. Kagan, "A Conception of Early Adolescence," 103.
7. R. D. Enright, D. K. Lapsley, and L. M. Olsen, "Early Adolescent Labor" in *The Journal of Early Adolescence* 5, no. 4 (Winter 1985): 402–3.
8. Elkind, *All Grown Up*, 4–5.
9. Search Institute, "Young Adolescents and Their Parents," 50–55.
10. Eda J. LeShan, *Sex and Your Teenager: A Guide for Parents* (New York: David McKay, 1969), 51.
11. James Dobson, *Preparing for Adolescence* (Santa Ana, Calif.: Vision House, 1978), 47.
12. Cited in *Homiletics* (April-June 1992): 34.
13. H. Stephen Glenn and Jane Nelsen, *Raising Children for Success* (Fair Oaks, Calif.: Sunrise Press, 1987), 27.
14. Elkind, *All Grown Up*, 204.

Chapter 4: A New Way of Thinking
1. L. Kohlberg and C. Gilligan, "The Adolescent as Philosopher," in *Twelve to Sixteen: Early Adolescence*, ed. Robert Coles, et al. (New York: W. W. Norton, 1972), 154.
2. Elkind, *All Grown Up*, 24.

3. David Elkind, "Understanding the Young Adolescent," *Adolescence* 13, no. 49 (Spring 1978): 127–34.
4. Ephron, *Teenage Romance*, 37.

Chapter 5: An Emotional Roller Coaster
1. James Dobson, *Parenting Isn't for Cowards* (Dallas: Word, 1987), 155.
2. For more information on logical consequences, see Jane Nelsen, *Positive Discipline* (New York: Ballantine Books, 1981, 1987).
3. Richard J. Foster, *Prayer: Finding the Heart's True Home* (San Francisco: HarperCollins, 1992), 3.
4. Bill Wennerholm, "Adolescence, The Bridge from Self-Esteem to Self-Esteem," *Changes* 1, no. 1 (Spring 1982): 3.
5. Glenn and Nelsen, *Raising Self-Reliant Children in a Self-Indulgent World*, 49.

Chapter 6: Finding a Personal Faith
1. Elkind, *All Grown Up*, 42.
2. Kagan, "A Conception of Early Adolescence," 93–94.
3. Frederick Buechner, *Wishful Thinking* (New York: Harper & Row, 1973), 20.
4. Elkind, *All Grown Up*, 42.
5. Search Institute, "Young Adolescents and Their Parents," 160.
6. Thomas H. Groome, *Christian Religious Education* (San Francisco: Harper & Row, 1980), 70. See also James Fowler, "Stages in Faith: The Structural-Developmental Approach," in *Values and Moral Development*, ed. Thomas C. Hennessy (New York: Paulist Press, 1976), 173 ff.
7. Elkind, *All Grown Up*, 40.
8. Benson et al., *The Quicksilver Years*, 89–103.
9. Howard and Stoumbis, *The Junior High and Middle School: Issues and Practices*, 34.